I0753102

THE

MORAVIAN MANUAL:

CONTAINING AN

ACCOUNT

OF THE

Protestant Church of the Moravian United Brethren,

OR

UNITAS FRATRUM.

BY

E. DE SCHWEINITZ,

PASTOR OF THE FRANKLIN STREET MORAVIAN CHURCH, PHILADELPHIA.

PUBLISHED BY AUTHORITY OF THE SYNOD, AND SANCTIONED BY THE PROVINCIAL BOARD.

PHILADELPHIA:

LINDSAY & BLAKISTON,

AND SOLD BY

A. M. SEIP, *Moravian Depository, No.* 557 *North Sixth Street;* G. W. PERKIN, *Moravian Bookstore, No.* 37 *Broad Street, Bethlehem, Pennsylvania;*
O. A. KEEHLN, *Moravian Depository, Salem, N. C.*

1859.

HENRY B. ASHMEAD, BOOK AND JOB PRINTER,
Sansom Street above Eleventh.

PREFACE.

The first Manual, giving an account of the Constitution and Discipline of the Moravian Church, was written by Bishop Spangenberg, and published in Germany, in the year 1774. In 1775, it was translated into English, and published in London, with a preface by the Rev. B. La Trobe. This work passed through a number of revised editions, both in the German and English languages. The last American edition, in a small pamphlet form of about seventy pages, appeared in 1833; but is now obsolete. It bears the following title: "A Concise Historical Account of the present Constitution of the Protestant Church of the United Brethren: Philadelphia, 1833." In the year 1789, a larger work, containing over three hundred and fifty pages, was written by the Rev. J. Loretz, and published in Germany, under the title: "Ratio Disciplinæ Unitatis Fratrum." The first part of this volume comprises an interesting sketch of the history of the Church; the other parts, treating of the Constitution and Discipline, are obsolete.

The Provincial Synod of the Northern District of the American Province, at its last meeting, held in the month of June,

1858, authorized the publication of a new Manual, suitable to the present wants of the Church in the United States, and committed the compilation of it to the writer. He has striven to fulfil the resolution adopted by the Synod, (see Journal of Synod of 1858, p. 105, F. 1,) to the best of his ability; although he found the duty assigned him a far more difficult one than he had supposed. The abundance of his materials often rendered it hard for him to decide what was essential, and what unessential; and the number of Synodical Journals and Reports to be consulted required the closest attention and considerable labor. Whatever the imperfections of the Manual may be, he thinks he can vouch for its authenticity.

The historical chapter contains an original sketch; and the chapter treating of the Present Condition of the Church is based upon the most recent information which could be obtained. In the Chapter on Doctrine, a Compendium will be found, setting forth the essential doctrines held by the Church. This Compendium has been drawn up with very great care, and exclusively in the language of authorized publications of the Church; excepting only the expression "we hold," which frequently occurs, or here and there a copulative, necessary to unite sentences derived from different works. The Compendium is therefore not a subjective treatise on Moravian Doctrine, but simply an authorized statement of it, compiled from Moravian books. For the remaining chapters, the following official documents were consulted: Results of the General Synod of 1848; Results of the General Synod of 1857; Report of the Proceedings of the Preparatory Provincial Conference, held at Bethlehem, Pa., in the month of

May, 1847; Report of the Proceedings of the Provincial Synod, held at Bethlehem, Pa., in the month of June, 1846; Journal of the Provincial Synod, held at Bethlehem, Pa., in the month of May, 1855; Journal of the Provincial Synod, held at Bethlehem, Pa., in the month of October, 1856: Digest of the Provincial Synod, held at Salem, N. C., in the month of May, 1856; Report of the Provincial Synod, held at Salem, N. C., in the month of February, 1858, as published in "The Moravian;" Journal of the Provincial Synod, held at Bethlehem, Pa., in the month of June, 1858. In drawing up the chapter on Constitution, the writer endeavored to present the entire Constitution, general and provincial, as explicitly, and in as symmetrical a form as possible. In order to effect this, it became necessary, when stating the statutes, to adopt one tense throughout, and he chose that which is commonly employed in constitutions. It has been his earnest endeavor not to omit a single point, belonging to the constitution; especially so far as the American Province is concerned. The Constitution of the Southern District was drawn up by a member of its Provincial Board.

This Manual was submitted, in manuscript, to the Provincial Board, at Bethlehem, Pa., and has received its sanction, after a careful examination of the contents. At the same time, however, it may be well to state, that the work is not intended, in any way at all, to *supersede* the "Results" of the last General Synod, or the Journals and Reports of the Provincial Synods of this Province. All these documents remain in force as heretofore, and will guide the deliberations of future Synods. The purpose of the Manual is a two-fold one: to give the members of the church, in one compendious volume, the ecclesiastical statutes, rules of discipline, and articles of doctrine, which heretofore could be found only by consulting a number of different publications;—and especially to afford an authentic work which may be put into the hands of such as seek information respecting the Moravian Church, and wish to become acquainted with its constitution, discipline, doctrine, and ritual.

The writer is indebted, for valuable statistics, to Bishop Wolle, of the Provincial Board at Bethlehem, to the Rev. G. F. Bahnson, of the Provincial Board at Salem, to the Rev. W. Mallalieu, of the British Provincial Board, and the Rev. L. T. Reichel, of the Unity's Elders' Conference.

Philadelphia, May 17, 1859.

PREFATORY NOTE.

The Church of which this volume treats is known by various names: *The United Brethren, The Moravian Church, The Church of the Moravian United Brethren, The Unitas Fratrum.* The latter name was adopted by the Ancient Church of the Brethren in the fifteenth century, and has been retained by the Renewed Church. It denotes all the Provinces and Missions of the Church, in whatever parts of the world they may be, as one confederated ecclesiastical body. A briefer appellation of the same import, is *The Unity*; and this is frequently used in the following work. The name *Moravian* is derived from the country of Moravia, where the Church formerly had some of its principal seats; and whence the men came by whom it was renewed in Saxony.

About the beginning of the present century, the followers of the Rev. W. Otterbein, who was originally a minister of the German Reformed Church, but left its communion, constituted themselves into a Society, which assumed the name of "United Brethren in Christ." This society is often confounded with the Church of the Moravian United Brethren. The two are distinct and separate denominations, in every respect.

The letters U. E. C. in this Manual, or in other Moravian works, stand for "Unity's Elders' Conference," the Executive Board administering the general government of the whole Church; the letters P. E. C. stand for "Provincial Elders' Conference," the Executive Board set over a particular Province of the Church. "Synodal Results" is the name by which the published Journal and Resolutions of the General Synod are commonly known.

CONTENTS.

CHAPTER VII.—DISCIPLINE.

STATISTICAL APPENDIX.

CORRECTION.

On page 54, to the list of churches in North Carolina, *Macedonia* should be added, which was commenced in 1856.

CHAPTER I.

HISTORY OF THE MORAVIAN UNITED BRETHREN'S CHURCH.

INTRODUCTION.

THERE are three eras in the history of the Moravian Church. The first comprises the period of the "Ancient Church," from the year 1457 to 1627; the second that of the "Hidden Seed," from which the Renewed Church has sprung, from the year 1627 to 1722; and the third that of the "Renewed Church," from the year 1722 to the present time. A brief sketch of the origin, progress, decline and renewal of the church is here presented. More complete histories are the following: *Cranz's Ancient and Modern History of the Brethren*, translated from the German by La Trobe, London, 1780; *Ratio Disciplinæ Unitatis Fratrum*, Barby, 1789; *Gedenktage der alten Bruederkirche*, Gnadau, 1821; *Bishop Holmes' History of the Brethren*, 2 vols., London, 1830; and *Bost's History of the Bohemian and Moravian Brethren*, published by the Religious Tract Society, London, 1848. Short sketches: *Historical Sketch of the Church and Missions of the United Brethren*, Bethlehem, 1848; and *Epitome of* *the History of the Church of the United Brethren*, Bradford, England, 1850. In the year 1842, a large number of original manuscripts were discovered, at Lissa, in Poland, relating to the Ancient Brethren's Church. These are now in the archives of Herrnhut, in Saxony, and known as the "Lissa Folios." They have thrown a new light upon the early history of the Brethren. Two eminent Bohemian historians have examined these records, and pronounce them invaluable both as regards the history of the church, and the general history of Bohemia and Moravia. The one is *Palacky*, who is giving the fruits of his researches in his great work, *Geschichte von Boehmen*, Prague, 1857, the fourth volume of which has appeared; the other, *Gindely*, whose work, *Geschichte der Boehmischen Brueder*, Prague, 1857, the second volume of which has been published, contains the most complete history of the Ancient Church that has been printed thus far;* although, being a Roman Catholic, his sentiments must be received with due caution. In the church itself, based upon the new sources, have appeared, *Kurze Darstellung der Geschichte der alten Boehmisch-Maehrischen Bruederkirche*, Rothenburg, 1852, by Henry Reichel, of Herrnhut; *Verbeek's kurzgefasste Geschichte der alten und neuen Brueder-Unitaet*, Gnadau, 1857; *Life of John Amos Comenius*, by D. Benham, Lon-

* *Plitt's Bruedergeschichte*, with additions and corrections by H. Reichel, is a voluminous and learned work, proceeding from the church itself; but remains in manuscript.

don, 1858. This work contains likewise an essay by Comenius, on the education of youth, entitled, "The School of Infancy." Histories of the Renewed Church exclusively are: *Croeger's Geschichte der erneuerten Bruederkirche*, 3 vols., Gnadau, 1854; *Memorial Days of the Renewed Brethren's Church*, 1822; *Schrautenbach's Graf v. Zinzendorf, und die Bruedergemeine seiner Zeit*, Gnadau, 1851—not a popular work, but setting forth what might be called the philosophy of the early history of the Renewed Church. The article in "Herzog's Real Encyclopædie," (or Bomberger's Condensed Translation,) on the Bohemian Brethren, is written from an ultra Lutheran point of view, without reference to the Lissa Folios, and does not present a truthful picture of the Ancient Church. In the "Encyclopedia Americana," there is an article on the United Brethren or Moravians, which has been copied into several histories of denominations. This article describes the church as it was when that work appeared; since which time its ecclesiastical constitution has undergone many changes. The "New American Cyclopædia" contains a correct account of the present church. In "Mosheim's Church History," a note by the translator, which the editor of the American edition has thought proper to retain, volunteers information respecting the Brethren, derived from one of the many scurrilous works, attacking and defaming the church, which were written by its bitter enemies, and published in the last century.

SECTION I.—THE ANCIENT CHURCH.

FROM 1457 TO 1627.

Bohemia and Moravia, once independent kingdoms, now provinces of the Austrian Empire, and strongholds of its Romish superstition, were the seats of the Ancient Brethren's Church. In the beginning of the ninth century, the Cheskian Slavonians, who at that time inhabited these countries, (having taken peaceable possession of them, in the fifth century, after the exodus of the Marcomanni,) and from whom the present race of Bohemians and Moravians are descended, were still dwelling in the darkness of heathenism. But about the middle of that century the light of Christianity arose upon them, partly through the instrumentality of the Roman Catholic, but chiefly through the exertions of the Greek Church. At the request of the Moravian Prince Rastislaw, himself a Christian, the Emperor Michael, in the year 863, sent two learned and zealous men from Constantinople, to preach the gospel to the people of Moravia. These were Cyrill and Methodius, brothers in the flesh, and "after the common faith," who became the apostles of the Bohemians and Moravians. In the year 871, the Prince of Bohemia, Boriwoy, and his wife, Ludmila, being on a visit to the Moravian court, embraced Christianity, and were baptized. This opened the way for the conversion of the Bohemian nation. Cyrill and Methodius, with the Bible in their hands, which the former had translated into the Slavonian tongue, established many churches in the two countries; everywhere introducing a Slavonian ritual. Thereby the foundation was laid for the national church-feeling and liberal principles which distinguished the Bohemians and Moravians, over against the pretensions of the Romish Hierarchy. The spirit of what was afterwards Protestantism manifested itself among them, and prepared the way for the Reformers before the Reformation. That the popes of Rome did not remain uninterested observers of these developments, may well be supposed. Every influence which they could exert was used to bring the Bohemian and Moravian church under their supremacy; and, at last, in the year 1079, the efforts of Gregory VII. were crowned with success. Bohemia and Moravia became parts of the Romish Hierarchy. However, the hearts of the people still clung to the customs of their fathers. They were ready, at any time, to welcome a reformer; and in the course of the next centuries, especially in the second half of the fourteenth, men arose among them who loved the truth, and approved themselves as forerunners of its great champion; through whom those principles were promulgated which led to the establishment of the Moravian Brethren's Church.

On the 6th of July, 1373, John Hus* was born, at

* This is the correct orthography of the name, according to the Cheskian. Huss is wrong. The name receives a second *s* in the genitive, like the Latin *os*, *ossis*. See Herzog's Encyclopædie, vol. vi. p. 324.

the village of Hussinetz, in the southern part of Bohemia. He was the apostle of the Brethren. Soon after having finished his studies at the University of Prague, he re-entered the institution as a teacher; and five years later was appointed professor of philosophy. Then God sent his Spirit, and Hus was converted. To understand the Scriptures now became the great purpose of his life; and he was determined not to be satisfied with systems of human philosophy. The writings of Wickliffe, which had found their way into Bohemia, and which he diligently studied, confirmed him in these resolutions. In the year 1402, Hus was appointed preacher of Bethlehem's church at Prague.* With great power and eloquence he began to attack the moral corruption prevailing among all classes, particularly the clergy. The indulgences, sold in 1412 by command of Pope John, in order to procure money for the war with the King of Naples, excited his deepest indignation; and he lifted up his voice against them until all Prague was moved, and the papal bull which granted them had been publicly burnt by the professors and students of the University. In consequence of this act, Hus was excommunicated, and religious services were forbidden in the city, as long as he should remain there. So he left Prague, and passed through the country,

* A wealthy citizen of Prague built this church, in spite of the opposition of the Romish Hierarchy, for the express purpose of giving a house of worship to the people, in which the gospel should be preached in the Cheskian and German languages.

everywhere preaching the word of God, and exposing the corruptions of the Romish Hierarchy. This was the seed-time of evangelical truth in Bohemia. The harvest came in its season. In the year 1414, a church-council assembled at Constance, in Switzerland. Hus was cited before this body. He obeyed the summons, relying on the safe-conduct granted him by the Emperor. But soon after his arrival he was treacherously imprisoned, and refusing to recant, unless his doctrines should be refuted from the Holy Scriptures, which the priests could not do, he was burnt alive, as a heretic, on the 6th of July, 1415, his forty-third birthday, and his ashes were cast into the Rhine. He met death with the holy courage of the early martyrs. In the following year, his intimate friend and coadjutor, Jerome of Prague, a layman, shared the same fate. The consequences of these acts of violence on the part of Rome, were fearful. Bohemia burned with fiery indignation. A powerful party, called the Hussites, flew to arms, and a most sanguinary contest ensued, known in history as the Hussite war. In the course of this war the principles and practice of Hus were often entirely forgotten by those who claimed to be his followers. They contended for political ends, besides those of religion; and were divided among themselves. Gradually two parties arose; the *Calixtines*, whose avowed purpose was the restoration of the cup, in the Lord's Supper, to the laity, (hence their name from *calix*, a cup,) and the *Taborites*, who demanded a general reformation of the church. The latter derived their name from a hill, called Mount Tabor, near Prague, on which they had their camp. They were the more enlightened of the two parties, and many who entertained their views disapproved entirely of a resort to arms. In the year 1431, the Council of Basle granted certain concessions to the Bohemians, known as the "Compacts of Basle." These were accepted by the Calixtines, but rejected by the Taborites. In consequence a civil war broke out between the two factions, and resulted in the total overthrow of the latter. The Calixtines now constituted the national church of Bohemia.

At its head stood Rokyzan, an eminent ecclesiastic; but not steadfast in the faith, wavering between his love for the truth and honor among men. This church soon became almost as corrupt as the Hierarchy; while the numerous sects which arose about that time, were distinguished for extravagant fanaticism rather than for sound doctrine or principles of true piety. To human eyes, a reformation of the church, and a revival of pure and undefiled religion, seemed farther off than ever. But God's time was come.

Amidst the general corruption to which the church returned, and the extravagances of the sects, there were those in Prague who deserved to be called Hussites in the true sense of the name; men of God, who had not taken up arms during the war, nor meddled with the subsequent political commotions of the country, nor given way to fanaticism; but held to the simple doctrines of the Bible, as expounded by Hus, and strove to live righteously and soberly, as he had taught. And in Bohemia and Moravia generally, many entertained and carried out similar principles, especially among those who had belonged to the more enlightened portion of the Taborites. No outward confederation existed among them. They were an invisible church. From the ranks of these men, God chose for himself the founders of the Church of the Brethren.

About the year 1450, Rokyzan, induced partly by his better convictions, but chiefly by his disappointment in not securing from the Pope the archbishopric of Bohemia, began to preach against the corruptions of the church, and to exhort the people to return to the pure principles of Hus. This gave new life to the men of God at Prague. They sought fellowship one with another, associated for the purpose of mutual edification, and gradually entered into connection with those of like mind in various parts of the country. A free religious Society imperceptibly came into being, at the head of which stood the brethren of Prague. The purpose of this Society was not only private edification, but a general reformation of the church, in which movement the awakened hoped that Rokyzan would take the lead. But their repeated requests to this effect were met with reserve, and finally refused altogether. Hence they withdrew, more and more, from the national church, particularly in the year 1454, and held to the priests among their own number. Rokyzan, although he did not fulfil their expectations, unwittingly became one of the principal instruments in the hand of God for the establishment of the church ordained by Him. Wearied by the importunities of these earnest inquirers after truth, he had advised them to read the works of Peter Chelcicky, an eminent and liberal lay-writer on religious subjects, and to seek his personal acqaintance. The views and sentiments of this man contributed very much to induce the momentous step which the associated brethren afterwards took, and by which they became an independent church. Nor was this all that Rokyzan did, in the way of preparation for such an issue, without dreaming that things were tending to it. Believing that it would be an easy method of getting rid of the men who were continually beseeching him to come out positively on the side of reformation, he obtained permission, in the year 1456, from George Podiebrad, Regent of Bohemia, for them to settle on an estate known as the barony of Lititz. It was the private property of the Regent, and lay in the northeastern part of Bohemia, in the circuit of Koenigingraetz, stretching to the confines of Glatz. But thinly populated at that time, its only villages were Zamberg or Senftenberg, Kunwalde, and Lititz. The latter was the seat of an ancient castle, on the river Adler. Its ruins are still to be seen, and on one of the gates is the inscription: "A. D. regnante Geo. Podiebrado 1468." This was the spot, by God's appointment, where the Moravian Brethren's Church should be founded.

A number of the awakened in the city of Prague embraced the permission granted by the Regent, and, in the same year, took up their abode at Kunwalde. The priest of Zamberg, Michael Bradacius by name, entertained the views of the more enlightened Taborites, was a true servant of the Lord, and sighed for a reformation of the church. This man, on the arrival of the brethren at Kunwalde, left his village and became their pastor. Many of their brethren after the faith gathered at the same place, from different parts of the country. And so a step had been taken which, in the providence of God, necessarily led to the establishment of a church.

The most eminent man of the association was Gregory, a nephew of Rokyzan—of strong faith, sound judgment, and holy living. He deserves to be called the patriarch of the Moravian Brethren's Church. By his advice, a more positive confederation came into being. The growing numbers of the awakened made this indispensable. Therefore the men of God at Kunwalde met in a solemn convention, in the year 1457, and drew up and adopted principles of doctrine and practice; constituting themselves, at the same time, into a regularly organized association, under the name of the "*Brethren and Sisters of the Law of Christ.*" Subsequently this name was changed to the simpler one of "*Brethren;*" and at a later period the title of "*Unitas Fratrum,*" or

"*Unity of the Brethren*," was adopted. Twenty-eight elders were chosen, some living on the estate of Lititz, but the most of them in other parts of Bohemia; who directed the association, and whom its members were to obey as those having the rule over them. Such was the first organization of the Moravian United Brethren's Church, four hundred and two years ago. The details of the event are wanting, because the Brethren intentionally concealed them at the time. The first of March is observed as the anniversary of the founding of the church; but there is no authority for supposing that the organization took place on that day. It is known for certain, however, that it was in the year 1457.

After this event, the Brethren lived in their retreat for some years, growing in grace and in the knowledge of the Scriptures. But in the year 1461, their numbers having greatly increased, and the events of 1457 becoming known, a fierce persecution broke out; and the foundations of the young church were bathed in the blood of many martyrs, who died rejoicing in Christ, like Hus before them. This was the first of a long series of oppressions which the Brethren suffered, and by which they were finally overwhelmed. In the present case, however, the rack and the stake only served to augment their numbers. Hence it became necessary to effect a still more complete organization. For this purpose a Synod was held, in the year 1464, at Lhota, a village on the estate adjoining the barony of Lititz. Seventy delegates assembled, and, in the first place, made the question of a total and final separation from the national church the subject of earnest deliberations. Having unanimously resolved to effect a separation, the Synod proceeded to elect from the twenty-eight elders appointed in 1457, three men to whom the government of the church should be entrusted. The choice fell upon Gregory, Procop, and John Klenowa. These men were not priests, but lay-elders. The ministerial functions were performed by Michael Bradacius, and other pastors, who had originally belonged to the Calixtine clergy, and been ordained by Calixtine bishops. However, as the Brethren could not hope to secure for the future a sufficiency of regular ministers, by secession from the national church, they convened another Synod, in the year 1467, again at Lhota, in order to take the important matter of the ministry into consideration. After much prayer, they left it to the decision of the Lord by lot, whether they should establish a ministry of their own; and if so, who should be set apart as candidates for ordination. They were guided in this use of the lot, by the example of the apostles, when choosing a successor to Judas Iscariot. The lot approved the establishing of an independent ministry; and designated Matthias of Kunwalde, Thomas of Przelautsch, and Elias of Krzizanow, as the candidates. But now another serious question arose. Who should ordain these men? The Synod believed that in the times of the apostles, there had been no difference between a bishop and a priest or presbyter, and that therefore the priests then present might at once proceed to the ordination. But, on the other hand, the assembled Brethren knew, that since a very early age, probably before the death of St. John, the last apostle, the church had commenced to make a distinction; and they were, above all, extremely solicitous to secure a ministry whose validity the Calixtines and Roman Catholics would be compelled to acknowledge. Hence they resolved to seek the episcopal succession. Now there were dwelling, in those days, on the confines of Bohemia and Austria, a colony of Waldenses. These, so the Synod was informed, had secured the regular episcopal succession; and their chief bishop, at that time, was Stephen. To him, therefore, the Synod sent a deputation, consisting of three priests or presbyters, namely, Michael Bradacius, a priest of the Roman Catholic, and a priest of the Waldensian Church, whose names have not been preserved—with instructions to lay before him a statement of what the Brethren had done, and to inquire into the validity of the Waldensian episcopate. Stephen received the deputies with great kindness, assembled his assistant bishops, and entered into a minute account of the episcopate which they had. The deputies, being fully satisfied, requested to be consecrated bishops, which request Stephen and his assistants fulfilled, in a solemn convocation of the Waldensian Church. The new bishops immediately returned to the barony of Lititz, where another Synod was convened, at which they set apart for the work of the ministry, by the laying on of hands, the three candidates previously appointed; consecrating Matthias a bishop, and ordaining Thomas and Elias presbyters. Thereupon a new form of church government was instituted. It consisted of a board or college of ten elders, some of whom were presbyters, and others laymen, at the head of which stood the four bishops, and at their head again Bishop Michael, who was the primate. This form of episcopal government, with slight modifications, remained until the end of the Ancient Church.

Thus was the Church of the Brethren, after ten years of gradual development, fully organized and established. In 1457, the foundation was laid, even that of the apostles and prophets, Jesus Christ himself being the chief corner-stone; in 1467, the topstone was put upon the building, in accordance with the directions given to the Brethren by the Lord himself. John Hus, the great Reformer of the fifteenth century, began the work; Rokyzan, the Calixtine bishop, without meaning to do so, furthered it; Peter Chelcicky, by his writings, gave it a more positive aim; Gregory, the patriarch of the Brethren, carried it out; and the Waldenses of Austria seem to have been preserved, as a distinct organization, that they might complete it; having done which, this colony of them passed away.*

* Soon after transferring the succession to the Brethren, Bishop Stephen was burnt at the stake, as a heretic, at Vienna.

In the years which followed these events, the Brethren, in spite of the persecutions to which they were subjected, increased numerically, and grew spiritually unto an holy temple in the Lord. Particular attention was paid to the discipline. It was their object to present, in this respect, the character of an apostolic church. About the year 1500, they had more than two hundred churches, in Bohemia and Moravia; were zealously engaged in preaching the gospel, and diligently used the press for the furtherance of evangelical truth; had published a Bohemian version of the Bible, several confessions of faith, and were preparing a hymn-book and catechism. The most distinguished man and writer among them, at this time, was Bishop Luke, of Prague, who did much to strengthen the church, in its doctrine and discipline; and their principal seats were Prerau, in Moravia, Jungbunzlau and Leitomischl, in Bohemia. At the latter places there were church printing establishments. From all this it appears, that the work which began sixty years before Luther nailed his theses to the door of the Wittenberg cathedral, had prospered greatly at the opening of the century in which he was to take his place on the stage of history; and assumed an importance, when he was yet unknown, which will ever award to the Brethren the title of *Reformers before the Reformation.* As such Luther himself acknowledged them, after he had become acquainted with their principles. And although there were points, especially in the discipline, in reference which he and the Brethren could not agree; nevertheless the relation between them, with some interruptions, was a friendly one. The Brethren sent several deputations to him; and he published their Seventh Confession of Faith, with a preface of his own, at Wittenberg. Still more cordial was the connection between the church and some of the other Reformers of the sixteenth century, especially Bucer and Calvin. That the Brethren were benefited by their intercourse with these leaders of the general Reformation, especially in a doctrinal point of view, admits of no doubt. But the latter, on their part, learnt many a lesson from the discipline of the Unitas, as Bucer, in particular, joyfully acknowledged.

Soon after Luther's death, the Smalcaldic war broke out, between the Catholics and Protestants. The Bohemians having refused to take part in it, Ferdinand, their king, brother of the Emperor Charles V., came to Prague, to wreak his vengeance upon the people; and as self-policy forbade him to molest the Calixtines, he began to persecute the Brethren. In 1548, a decree was promulgated, commanding all persons living on royal estates to join either the Calixtine or Romish Church, or to leave the country within forty-two days. A large number of the members of the Brethren's Church, residing on such estates, emigrated, in consequence, and took their way to Prussia. Meanwhile the Brethren had extended their operations to Poland. George Israel, the patriarch of the Unitas in that country, labored with great success; so that in a period of less than six years, about forty churches were established among a people who had almost exclusively been Roman Catholics. These churches were strengthened afterwards, by the arrival of the Brethren who had gone to Prussia; for being oppressed there most shamefully by bigoted Lutherans, they sought refuge in Poland. In this way the Unitas Fratrum extended more and more, and gradually came to consist of three confederated provinces—the Bohemian, Moravian and Polish. These provinces had bishops and synods of their own, but remained closely united as one church, and together held general synods. The first synod of this kind took place in 1557, the centennial year of the existence of the church, and was convened at Slecza, in Moravia. Seven years later the outward prosperity of the Brethren in Bohemia and Moravia increased greatly; for in common with the other Protestants of these countries, they enjoyed the favor of the liberal monarch who ascended the throne at that time, under the title of Maximilian II. In connection with the Lutherans and Reformed, they formed an Evangelical Church Union, whose united influence gave them rest and peace. Hence their cause prospered very much, in some respects. They increased more and more, and numbered many of the noblest and most influential families of Bohemia and Moravia among their members; they established theological seminaries and developed their ecclesiastical resources in many other particulars, publishing amongst the rest, the celebrated Bohemian Bible of Cralitz, translated from the original, by their bishops, after a labor of fifteen years, and printed in six folio volumes. At the same time, however, their spiritual welfare suffered; and their discipline was relaxed. In the year 1609, the Emperor Rudolph II. was constrained to establish permanently the liberties which the evangelical party had enjoyed under Maximilian, by the promulgation of his well-known "letters of majesty." And so the Unitas Fratrum, which had been founded in great humility, became a legally acknowledged church of the land; held as its own Bethlehem's chapel at Prague, where Hus, its original apostle, had proclaimed the gospel; and had a bishop associated with the administrator of the Evangelical Consistory. But from this pinnacle of outward prosperity, the church of the Brethren, in the inscrutable providence of God, was to fall into the depths of adversity, in common with the other Protestant denominations of the country.

Rudolph was succeeded by Matthias; and in the event of his death, Ferdinand of Tyrol, the personification of Romish bigotry, would be king. Hence the evangelical party determined to set him aside, and in 1619, when Matthias died, elected Frederick of the Palatinate, a Protestant prince, to the throne of Bohemia. But Ferdinand completely overthrew his power, the very next year. Having done this, he set as the great purpose of his life, the total and permanent extinction of evangelical truth in Bohemia and Moravia. By his directions, an Anti-Reformation was undertaken,* of which Jesuits and Capuchins were the heralds, and imperial dragoons the champions. It began, in 1621, at Prague, with the execution of twenty-seven noblemen, several of whom were members of the Brethren's Church; and in the course of the next six years, was carried into every part of the two countries. The fundamental principle of this Anti-Reformation was: "Abjure evangelical faith, or leave the country." More than thirty thousand Bohemians and Moravians emigrated. The sanctuaries of the Brethren, of the Lutherans and of the Reformed, were closed; their congregations scattered, and as sheep without a shepherd, wandered from place to place; the evangelical party in Moravia and Bohemia ceased to exist. And ever since that time, these countries have remained among the darkest of Romish lands. When the year 1627 dawned, the Moravian-Bohemian branch of the Unitas Fratrum was no more. The Polish branch continued for a period longer. But being deprived of the strength of the main stem, it was gradually grafted upon the Reformed Church of Poland, and in the next decades grew to be one with it. This came to

* We take pleasure in referring the reader to Dr. Pescheck's interesting work, "Reformation and Anti-Reformation in Bohemia," published in London, or to the original, "Pescheck's Geschichte der Gegenreformation in Boehmen," Leipzig, 1850.

pass the more readily, because the Brethren had always been actuated by a sincere spirit of union, in their intercourse with other evangelical Christians; and as early as 1570, had succeeded in effecting a visible manifestation of this spirit—a kind of "Evangelical Alliance"—at the celebrated Synod of Sendomir, in Poland; a convention composed of representatives of the Unitas Fratrum, of the Lutheran and the Reformed Churches, which unitedly issued the *Consensus Sendomiriensis.*

And so the enemies of the venerable Unitas, founded a century and three-quarters of a century before, had to all appearances accomplished a final triumph. But in reality the victory was only a temporary one. The church was cast down, not destroyed. A Hidden Seed remained.

SECTION II.—THE HIDDEN SEED.

FROM 1627 TO 1722.

The history of the Hidden Seed, from which the Renewed Moravian Brethren's Church has sprung, belongs to the mysterious ways in which God moves "His wonders to perform," and is a glorious fulfilment of His prediction, that against His church the gates of hell shall not prevail. It sets forth the faith and hopes of a man of God, who may be called the Jeremiah of the Ancient Church, and the John the Baptist of the Renewed, and what he did in the strength of that faith and by the elevating power of those hopes; and it brings to our notice the traditions and principles of old, as preserved for ninety-four years among the descendants of the Brethren, in single families, which were in spiritual bondage, but like the Jewish exiles in Babylon, could not forget their Jerusalem.

John Amos Comenius (born March 28th, 1592, in Moravia,) was the man whom God had appointed to prepare the way for the renewal of the church. The seed which fell from the tree planted by Gregory and his coadjutors, in the middle of the fifteenth century, nurtured and pruned by Luke of Prague and his brother bishops in the beginning of the sixteenth, and then cut down by the ruthless hand of persecution, in the second quarter of the seventeenth, was fostered with great care by Comenius, and watered with many tears, until, in the providence of God, Zinzendorf re-planted it in a new soil, in the eighteenth century, where it took root, and has now grown up a second tree, whose branches extend to the far parts of the earth.

Comenius, after having studied at a German university, was appointed, in 1616, Rector of the Brethren's seminary, and pastor of the church at Prerau, in Moravia. Two years later he filled the same offices at Fulneck, until this place was destroyed by Spanish soldiers. In the year 1627, in company with a number of his brethren, he proceeded to Lissa, in Poland. On their way thither, having reached the summit of the mountain-ridge which separates Silesia and Bohemia, they fell down upon their knees, and Comenius prayed most fervently, with strong cries and tears, that God would not take his Word entirely away from Bohemia and Moravia, but preserve unto himself a seed in these countries. From that day a prophetical anticipation of the renewal of the Brethren's Church, filled his soul. In the year 1632, a Synod, composed of fugitive ministers and members of the Moravian-Bohemian branch of the Unity, was held at Lissa, on which occasion Comenius was consecrated bishop of that branch of the church. The hopes of the scattered Brethren, at this time, were high, that the Protestant arms would prove victorious in the thirty years war, which was raging; and that the restoration of the church in the countries from which it had been uprooted, would soon be accomplished. In this expectation, however, Comenius and his brethren were mistaken. The peace of Westphalia was concluded in 1648, but Bohemia and Moravia continued wholly in the power of Rome; and the fruits of the Reformation before the Reformation commenced by Hus, had, indeed, so far as these countries were concerned, effectually and permanently been destroyed. And yet the prayer of Comenius did not remain unfulfilled. There was a seed of righteousness hidden in his native land, and it should become manifest in God's own time, but in a manner different from what he anticipated. Meanwhile this servant of the Lord had been visiting various parts of Germany, Sweden and England, in the interests of the cause of education, which engaged his warmest sympathy. He returned to Lissa in the year 1648. Eight years afterwards, when the town was destroyed by the Cossacks, he and the Brethren who had been living there, left it finally. The latter were scattered over different countries. Comenius, after a short abode at Frankfort on the Oder, proceeded to Amsterdam, and remained there for the rest of his life, engaged in literary labors. His writings were very numerous, and some of them celebrated in their day; for instance, *Janua Linguarum Reserata*, (published in 1631,) which was translated into twelve European and several Asiatic languages. In the year 1671, after having acknowledged and bewailed the errors into which he had fallen at one period of his life, in consequence of his connection with persons who claimed to receive revelations from God, this venerable servant of the Most High, the last bishop of the Moravian-Bohemian line, ended his eventful career in the seventy-ninth year of his age, hoping still for the restoration of the Unitas Fratrum. For this end he had never ceased to work in all the countries which he had visited, and especially during his long exile in Holland. The most important and abiding results of these labors may be summed up as follows: First, he republished the discipline and church-order of the Brethren, adding a history of the church and reflections of his own,—the whole work bearing the title, *Ratio Disciplinæ Ordinisque Ecclesiastici in Unitate Fratrum Bohemorum*, and dedicated it to the Church of England, to which he also solemnly commended the Unity of the Brethren in the event of its renewal. Again, he published a Catechism, containing the doctrines of the church, and dedicated it "To all the godly sheep of Christ, dispersed here and there, especially to those of Fulneck, Gersdorf, Glandorf, Klitte, Kunwalde, Stachewald, Seitendorf, and Zauchtenthal," villages of Moravia, where many Brethren still dwelt, and from each of which, in the next century, emigrants came to Herrnhut. And, finally, he cared for the preservation of the episcopate, and in the year 1662 took measures for the consecration of two new bishops, in hope against hope. These were Nicholas Gertichius, court-chaplain of the Duke of Liegnitz, and Peter Jablonsky, pastor of a church at Danzig. Through them the succession was carefully preserved until the year 1735, when it was transferred to the Renewed Church of the Brethren.

And now we pass to the history proper of the Hidden Seed. It is soon told. The Anti-Reformation in Bohemia and Moravia, under Ferdinand II., was at an end, the Brethren's Church extinct, and these countries lay, in abject submission, at the feet of Rome; but in the very nature of the case, many families had been forced into a mere outward conformity to the Romish worship, without yielding the convictions of their hearts. This was particularly so among the members of the Unitas Fratrum who had remained in their native land. They were true to the doctrines of their fathers, in so far as they could be, under the oppression of the Hierarchy; they had carefully concealed their bibles, hymn-books, and other evangelical writings; strengthened their faith by these means, and often met, in secret, for mutual edification, as the founders of the church had done two centuries before. Occasionally they were visited by exiled pastors, who administered the Lord's Supper to them; at other times they went on journeys to Protestant countries, and received the sacrament there. All this was done with the utmost secrecy; and if any were discovered by the Romish priests engaged in such devotions, they were severely punished. For a series of years, this state of affairs continued. Towards the close of the seventeenth century, when a new generation had grown up, the light of evangelical truth was obscured among the descendants of the Brethren; still, the traditions and principles of former days remained in single families, especially in Moravia, and the Unitas Fratrum was never entirely forgotten. There were, in particular, individual men of God,—aged fathers of the invisible church,—who kept up the connection between the present and the past, and looked with longing eyes into the future. Among these, Martin Schneider, of Zauchtenthal, and after him, his grandson, Samuel Schneider, deserve to be mentioned,—both of whom were preachers of righteousness in their families and among their neighbors, and ceased not to exhort to repentance, and to encourage the hope of a resuscitation of the Church of the Brethren. No less distinguished, in this respect, was George Jaeschke, of Sehlen. Born 1624, in the midst of the oppressions of the Anti-Reformation, by which the Unitas Fratrum was overwhelmed, trained up with pious solicitude in the ways of the Lord, and taught to love the principles of evangelical truth, he lived for more than four-score years, from the beginning almost to the end of the period of the Hidden Seed, doing what he could to perpetuate the memory of the fathers, and keep alive their faith. This man had five grandsons, of the family of the Neissers, and a young son, Michael by name, born to him in his extreme old age. In the year 1707, feeling his departure to be at hand, he called his son and grandsons around his bed, laid upon them his blessing, commending Michael to the particular care of the latter; and then, full of faith, which seemed to catch something of the spirit of prophecy, as he drew near the land of sight, declared it to be his firm conviction that the time for a renewal of the Brethren's Church was close at hand; exhorting them not to hesitate to make any sacrifices in view of this event, even if it should be to forsake their homes and native country. And so he died. But, however bright the anticipations of this patriarch were, they seemed destined not to be fulfilled; for when he was no more, and when the Schneiders and other fathers were gone, the meetings for edification which they had held, were gradually given up, or restricted to family worship. The reading of evangelical books, the singing of Brethren's hymns, and other similar exercises, were, indeed, continued by their descendants, but as meritorious works, in which, together with the rejection of Romish superstitions, they sought the essence of evangelical piety, instead of cultivating repentance, faith and holiness. Humanly speaking, therefore, the Hidden Seed seemed on the point of perishing forever; and the prospect of a resuscitation of the Unitas Fratrum farther off than at any previous period. But this was God's time. Fifteen years after the aged Jaeschke had been gathered to his fathers, his dying anticipations, and the prayer of Comenius before him, uttered on the mountain-top, began to be fulfilled. The days came for the re-planting of the Hidden Seed. The history of the Renewed Brethren's Church opens.

SECTION III.—THE RENEWED CHURCH.

FROM 1722 TO 1859.

The renewal of the church was not a work of man, but of God. No well devised plan, no fixed purpose, except to glorify His name, actuated the agents whom He employed. They were led by a way they knew not, step by step, even as the founders of the Ancient Unitas had been, until the work was accomplished, and the old principles rejuvenated by the infusion of new life from the Evangelical Church of Germany, beat with great throbs in a new body ecclesiastic, and were felt in distant countries, and among heathen tribes.

A glance at the preparations made in Germany for

the renewal of the church, unknowingly to those engaged in them, will first be necessary.

In the second half of the seventeenth century, God called a man to the service of the Evangelical Church of Germany, who built with great zeal upon the foundation laid by the Reformers, and accomplished a work which they did not live long enough to perform. His name was Philip Jacob Spener, born in 1635, died in 1705. He recognized the importance of awakening more spirituality among Christians, and directed all his efforts to this end; upholding, in particular, the idea of what he called *ecclesiolae in ecclesia*—little churches within the church—composed of converted Christians, and having for their aim the furtherance of personal piety, and the purifying and sanctifying of the whole church. In the beginning of the eighteenth century, there lived at Hennersdorf, an estate of Upper Lusatia, in Saxony, a learned and godly woman, the Baroness de Gersdorf, who had adopted this idea of Spener, and carried it out in her own immediate circle. On the 26th of May, her daughter, who had married a Count of Zinzendorf, gave birth to a son, who received the name of Nicholas Lewis. His father, who filled a high office at the Saxon court, died soon after, and his education was committed to the care of his grandmother, who took him to her estate, and procured for him a pious and excellent instructor, named Edeling. Under these influences, Zinzendorf grew up and learned to love the Lord with his whole heart, from his earliest infancy. After having made a covenant, which had for its aim the spread of the gospel, with several friends, particularly with Baron Frederick de Watteville, while pursuing his studies at the University; he purchased the estate of Berthelsdorf, on attaining to his majority, in order to make it the centre from which to extend his operations on behalf of Christ's cause. In what particular manner these operations should be carried on, he, as yet, knew not. In the year 1722, Andrew Rothe, a devoted young clergyman, became the parish-minister of this estate, by the vocation of Zinzendorf. A few months later, the Count married Erdmuth Dorothea, Countess of Reuss, a true handmaid of Jesus, who was ready to second all her husband's efforts for the furtherance of the kingdom of God. At that time there lived in the town of Goerlitz, about a half day's journey from Berthelsdorf, a faithful minister of Christ, Schaeffer by name, united with Zinzendorf in the closest bonds of friendship, and sharing his desire to promote the cause of the Lord; and an humble mechanic, called Christian David, a native of Moravia, once a bigoted Romanist, now, after many outward trials and inward agonies, brought to a full knowledge of the truth as it is in Jesus, mainly through Schaeffer's instrumentality.

These were the agents by whom the Lord God was about to renew the days of the Brethren as of old; and such the preparations which had been going on for the resuscitation of their church.

Christian David had "faith which worketh by

love." Himself rejoicing in the Lord, he longed to make others the partakers of his joy. And so, in the years from 1717 to 1722, he undertook several journeys into Moravia, visiting the former seats of the Brethren, and preaching Christ Jesus and Him Crucified. An awakening took place, in consequence, among those who were evangelically predisposed, and especially in the families descended from the Brethren. Some of these expressed a strong desire to seek a home elsewhere, that they might enjoy liberty of conscience. Christian David came and went several times, without finding for them such a home. But as often as he returned to Goerlitz, he spoke of their wishes. Schaeffer became interested in the case, and reported it to Rothe; Rothe mentioned it to Zinzendorf, and Zinzendorf sent for Christian David. The result of the conversation between them was an invitation to the awakened, on the part of the former, to come to Berthelsdorf, where they should find a retreat until they could secure a better place of abode. This was in 1722. On Whit-Monday of that year, Christian David suddenly re-appeared among his friends in Moravia, when they had given up the hope of ever seeing him again, and brought them the message of the Count. Thereupon two of the grandsons of the patriarch Jaeschke, Jacob and August in Neisser, immediately determined to emigrate. On Wednesday, the 27th day of May, at 10 o'clock at night, these two men, their wives and four children, a young girl who was a relative of the family, and

Michael Jaeschke, whom their grandfather had so earnestly commended to their care in the event of an emigration—ten souls in all—left house and home for Christ's sake, and led by Christian David, safely crossed the frontier. By way of Goerlitz, where Schaeffer welcomed and greatly encouraged them, they arrived at Berthelsdorf on the eighth of June. Nine days later, this little company assembled in a wood of the estate, bordering on the high-road from Loebau to Zittau, in order to begin the erection of a house. The spot was a dreary wilderness, but Christian David, full of faith, struck his axe into a tree and exclaimed, "Here the sparrow hath found a house, and the swallow a nest for herself, where she may lay her young, even thine altars, O Lord of Hosts, my King and my God." (Ps. 84:3.) Such was the beginning of Herrnhut, the mother-church of the Renewed Unitas Fratrum.

In the month of November of the same year, the house was dedicated in a solemn manner; on which occasion Christian David declared it to be his conviction, that a city of God would there arise, whose light would shine far and wide. All these events took place under the direction of Count Zinzendorf's steward, Heiz by name, a man of faith and of God. The Count himself was absent, having accepted a post at the Saxon court, contrary to his own inclinations, but in obedience to the will of his family. In the month of December, when on his way to Hennersdorf, with his young bride and his friend, Baron de Wattewille, as the carriage passed the spot where Herrnhut now stands, he saw a new house erected near the road. On inquiring of his servants, he learned that the immigrants from Moravia lived there. Zinzendorf alighted from the carriage, and entered the humble abode. That was the first meeting between the Moravian Brethren and the man whom God had ordained to be the chief agent in the renewal of their ancient church.

At that time, however, the Count had no idea of such a thing. He had merely given shelter to a few homeless wanderers. His plan was, without any reference to them, to form on his estate an *ecclesiola in ecclesia,* of which he, Wattewille, Rothe, and Schaeffer, should be the leaders, and through this association to work for the spread of the gospel. And this purpose he pursued for a time, paying but little attention to the immigrants. But his thoughts were not God's thoughts. The number of Moravian Brethren increased rapidly, for Christian David repeatedly visited his native country, and family after family followed him to Saxony. By and by, awakened persons from Germany were attracted to Herrnhut, and in the short period of five years, a colony was gathered on Zinzendorf's estate, numbering upwards of three hundred souls.

Meanwhile the Adversary had not been idle. Dissensions broke out among them. The Moravians insisted on introducing the ancient discipline of their fathers; those not from Moravia knew nothing of it.

In points of doctrine too, there was much dispute. This state of affairs continued for two years. But in 1727, Zinzendorf, who had made the colony the subject of his daily prayers, came to Herrnhut for the purpose of effecting a change for the better. Several of the leading brethren were called together, and with their assistance, he drew up statutes, based upon the ancient discipline of the Brethren, so far as this was known. These statutes were solemnly adopted on May 12th, and the inhabitants of Herrnhut pledged themselves to observe them. In this way, peace and harmony were restored. Soon after, Zinzendorf found, in the library of Zittau, a copy of the *Ratio Disciplinæ** of the Unitas Fratrum, published by Comenius in the event of the renewal of the church; translated the work, while on a journey, and brought it to Herrnhut, to the great joy of the Moravians, whose ancient discipline was now restored.

The events of the month of May were sealed by God himself, on the occasion of a general celebration of the Lord's Supper, in the parish church of Berthelsdorf, when the Brethren of Herrnhut were baptized with the Holy Ghost, in a most abundant manner, and amid a general melting together of hearts, covenanted before the Lord to be and remain one in Him. This day (August 13th) was the spiritual birthday of the Renewed Brethren's Church, and is commemorated as such.

* This copy is still to be seen at Zittau, together with the letter of the Count, returning thanks for the loan of it.

The remainder of the history must be given very briefly. The reader is referred to larger works on the subject; particularly to a translation of Croeger's History.

From that day on, the cause of the Brethren prospered greatly, in the face of much opposition and persecution; and the will of the Lord, that the Ancient Unitas Fratrum should be renewed, was manifested more and more plainly, in spite of Zinzendorf's great reluctance to accept this idea; until the renewal was consummated by the transfer of the episcopate, which had been so wonderfully preserved, in hope against hope, to the Brethren of Herrnhut. In the year 1735, March 13th, David Nitschmann, a Moravian immigrant, was consecrated the first bishop of the Renewed Brethren's Church, by Daniel Jablonsky and Christian Sitkovius, the surviving bishops of the ancient succession. The second bishop was Count Zinzendorf himself, who had resigned his office at the Saxon court, and, relinquishing all worldly honors, given himself up entirely to the ministry of the gospel, and the service of the Brethren. Thus the Renewed Brethren's Church was fully organized; and the faith and hopes of the venerable Comenius were abundantly realized. In the course of the next years, the church was recognized by the governments of Prussia and Saxony, and by the parliament of Great Britain, which also acknowledged the validity of the episcopate. Concessions were afterwards granted in all the countries of Europe, to which the church spread.

Meanwhile the particular purpose for which the Lord had brought about this renewal, was already being carried out. It was the work of foreign missions. In the year 1732, the first missionaries went forth from Herrnhut, only one decade after its founding; and since that time, this has been the field to which the church has directed its chief attention, and devoted its strength. Soon not only a Renewed Church, but a second Unitas Fratrum, in the full sense of the words, was established. Churches arose in Great Britain, where the Brethren, in the providence of God, exercised considerable influence upon the founders of Methodism, and gave to them various fundamental principles, which have since been fully developed in the Methodist Church; and in North America, where the conversion of the Indian tribes engaged their zealous attention for many years, and was crowned with great success. In this way three provinces came into being, the Continental, British and American; corresponding to the Moravian, Bohemian and Polish, of the Ancient Church. A very extensive home mission work, on the Continent of Europe, was also commenced, which is known by the name of the *Diaspora*. The fundamental principle which guided Zinzendorf in all his operations on the home field of the three provinces, even after the full reorganization of the Ancient Church, was Spener's idea of a church within the church. To the realization of this, all the peculiar arrangements and regulations of the settlements of the Brethren tended.

Each settlement was not only a church, but a religious community, governed by laws having for their object a total separation from the sinful follies and carnal lusts of the world. This served to keep the church numerically small; but also to foster the spirit of missionary zeal, which constrained the Brethren to go to the most degraded nations of the earth, and caused their congregations from among the heathen to multiply greatly. At the same time, the truth as it is in Jesus, the simple gospel of a Crucified Saviour, was preserved in the midst of the settlements; and, as has well been observed by a modern church-historian,* however little we agree with some other of his views respecting the Brethren: "In the era of infidelity, the Christ of the fathers had a sanctuary at Herrnhut."

As long as Zinzendorf lived, the government of the church, in a great measure, depended upon him. Two of his most distinguished assistants were his son-in-law, Baron John de Wattewille, and Augustus Spangenberg, both bishops of the church. The merits of the latter were particularly great, as the pioneer of the church in America, and as a theologian. After Zinzendorf's death, which took place in 1760, a more positive ecclesiastical constitution was adopted. The Synods received the supreme power; and the executive administration of the affairs of the church was committed to an elective college or board of bishops and elders, which in 1769 took the title of the

* Dr. Hase, in his Kirchengeschichte.

"Unity's Elders' Conference." Subordinate boards were appointed for the superintendence of the American and British Provinces. In the year 1822, the Renewed Unitas Fratrum celebrated its centennial anniversary. Since that period preparations for a change in some of its principles silently began. These preparations showed themselves particularly in the American Province. The idea of a church within the church, was relinquished more and more; the majority of the American congregations never having been "settlements." In consequence the necessity of provincial self-government was felt; and responded to, in some degree, by the General Synod of 1848. It remained, however, for the General Synod of 1857 to effect a complete remodeling of the constitution. The three provinces are now independent in local and provincial concerns, but closely confederated in all general principles of doctrine and practice, and in the work of foreign missions. In the same year in which these changes were accomplished, the Moravian Brethren, on the first of March, celebrated the fourth centennial anniversary of the first organization of their church, on the barony of Lititz, in 1457; and with humility, yet exceeding great joy, in the United States, on the Continent of Europe, in Great Britain, and in all their many mission churches, covenanted anew with the God of their fathers, to be His people, even as they had faith in Him, that He would continue to be their God.

CHAPTER II.

PRESENT CONDITION OF THE CHURCH.

THE Moravian Brethren's Unity, at the present time, is divided into three provinces: known as the *American*, comprising the Moravian churches in the United States; the *Continental*, embracing those on the Continent of Europe; and the *British*, to which those in Great Britain and Ireland belong. In this chapter, an account of each province, together with its enterprises, is given; as also of the cause in which the whole Unity is engaged.

SECTION I.—THE AMERICAN PROVINCE.

The American Province contains two districts, the *Northern* and *Southern*. To the latter belong the Moravian churches in North Carolina; to the former, all the rest in the United States. Each district has a government of its own, consisting of a Synod and Provincial Board; but the closest union exists between the two.

Formerly there were several church-settlements in the American Province, but the peculiar ecclesiastical polity which made them such, has been relinquished, the towns have been thrown open to all who may choose to settle in them, and the Moravian churches of America, without exception, are now ordinary churches, like those of other denominations. The establishments known as Brethren's, Sisters', and Widows' Houses, have likewise been given up.

The following are the churches of the American Province:

PENNSYLVANIA. — *Bethlehem*, in Northampton County, formerly a church-settlement, now an incorporated borough, the mother congregation of the Brethren in America, begun in 1741, organized in 1742. It is the seat of the Provincial Board, of the General Home Mission Board, of the Moravian College and Theological Seminary, and of a Church Boarding School for young ladies. The Moravian Book Store and Publication Office are also located here. *Nazareth*, in Northampton County, formerly a church-settlement, now an incorporated borough, begun in 1744, organized in 1747, the seat of the Moravian Classical Seminary and Boarding School for boys. *Schoeneck*, in Northampton County, begun in 1757, organized in 1763. *Emmaus*, in Lehigh County, begun in 1742, organized in 1747. *Hopedale*, in Wayne County, begun in 1834, organized in 1837. *Philadelphia*, (church edifice at the corner of Franklin and Wood streets,) begun in 1742, organized in 1749. *Litiz*, in Lancaster County, formerly a church-settlement, now an incorporated borough, begun in 1743, organized in 1756, the seat of a Church Boarding School for young ladies. *Lancaster City*, begun in 1748, organized in 1750.

York, in York County, begun in 1744, organized in 1755. *Lebanon*, in Lebanon County, organized in 1847.

NEW YORK.—*New York City*, (church edifice on Houston street, corner of Mott,) begun in 1742, organized in 1748. *Brooklyn*, (church edifice corner of Jay and Myrtle streets,) organized in 1854. *Staten Island*, begun in 1747, organized in 1763. *Camden*, in Washington County, begun in 1830, organized in 1834.

MARYLAND.—*Graceham*, in Frederick County, begun in 1745, organized in 1758.

OHIO.—*Gnadenhuetten*, begun in 1797, organized in 1799. *Fry's Valley*, organized in 1858. *Sharon*, begun in 1810, organized in 1827. *Canal Dover*, begun in 1840, organized in 1842. All these churches are in Tuscarwas County.

INDIANA.—*Hope*, in Bartholomew County, begun in 1825, organized in 1830.

ILLINOIS.—*West Salem*, in Edward's County, organized in 1844; divided into two churches, an English and a German one, in 1858.

WISCONSIN.—*Watertown* and *Ebenzer*, in Jefferson County, begun in 1853, organized in 1858.

NORTH CAROLINA.—*Salem*, formerly a church-settlement, now an incorporated borough, organized in 1766, the seat of the Provincial Board of the Southern District, and of a Church Boarding School for young ladies. An African church is located here. *Bethabara*, organized in 1753. *Bethania*, organized in 1760. *Friedberg*, organized in 1766. *Friedland*, organized in 1780. *Hope*, organized in 1780. *New Philadelphia*, organized in 1846. *Mount Bethel*, organized in 1851. *Muddy Creek*, organized in 1856. All these churches are in Davidson and Forsyth Counties.

Enterprises of the American Province.

A. THE HOME MISSION.—This is the name given to the work recently commenced by the church in different parts of the United States, among such as are destitute of the gospel privileges. It has respect chiefly, although not exclusively, to German immigrants. The initiatory steps in the enterprise were taken after the Provincial Synod of 1849, when the Province had been put upon a more independent footing. At the next Synod, in 1855, a regular plan of operations was matured, and a General Home Mission Board elected, composed of eight members, besides the members of the Provincial Elders' Conference. (See next chapter.) This Board appoints the missionaries, and directs the entire work. It is supported by voluntary contributions, collected through the agency of Home Mission Societies, of which there are a number in the different churches of the Province. There is no funded capital whatever at the disposal of the Board. Some of the Societies maintain one or more missionaries, without any assistance from the general treasury.

At the Provincial Synod of 1858, certain principles, regulating the enterprise, were adopted, whereof the following is an abstract, which will set forth the nature of the work. (See Journal of Synod, page 108.)

1. The great object of our Moravian Home Mission is to spread the gospel, and above all to win souls for Jesus, where-ever He opens the door in our country, and to form societies and congregations in full communion with the Moravian Church.

2. The Home Mission Board is authorized to appoint a Missionary for any Home Mission Society, which shall provide, to the satisfaction of said Board, the necessary means for the support of such Home Missionary.

3. Any number of persons may, with the written consent of the Home Mission Board, and under such rules and regulations as said Board shall prescribe, organize themselves into a "Moravian Home Missionary Congregation," the members of which shall be considered members of the Brethren's Church.

4. In case that a Home Mission Society deem it expedient that their Missionary be removed, and another appointed in his place, said society is expected to make application to this end to the H. M. Board, in order that the proposed change in the ministry may be made only after a thorough investigation of the grievances complained of.

5. It is the duty of our Home Missionaries to organize their stated hearers, as soon as may be, into associations for the maintenance of worship according to the Moravian ritual, and for the observance of Christian rules of order, as they may be laid down by the "Home Mission Board."

6. Such association standing in connection with, and under the auspices of our branch of the Moravian United Brethren's Church, shall be called a "Moravian Home Mission Congregation," and the sacraments may be administered to its mem-

bers, if otherwise they possess the requisite qualifications for a worthy participation in the same.

7. When such Home Mission Congregation shall have been completely organized, and its members fully instructed and indoctrinated in the views and principles of our church, said H. M. Congregation may be constituted a regular Brethren's Church, in accordance with the requisitions laid down by the General and Provincial Synods.

8. In all cases prior to the organization of a new Brethren's Church, a written application, signed by those who apply for such organization, must be sent to the H. M. Board, who, if they deem proper, shall proceed to organize the H. M. Congregation so applying, into a regular Moravian Church.

9. A Moravian Church gathered in the Home Mission field shall not be entitled to representation in the Provincial Synods, until it is able to maintain and support a minister out of its resources; provided, however, that two or more contiguous churches, under the care of one minister, may unite in an application to be represented in Synod, and such congregations shall unitedly be entitled to one delegate.

10. All applications for admission into the class of churches represented in Synod, shall be made in writing, through the Home Mission Board, to the Synod itself, which is the only body that shall have power to grant such admission.

11. No person shall be employed as a Missionary, unless he shall be well acquainted with the doctrines, history, principles, and discipline of the Brethren's Church, and shall have been a member of the Church for at least one year preceding his appointment.

12. When a Missionary shall have been ordained a Deacon, and subsequently served at least six years, and shall have, in the opinion of the Home Mission Board, approved himself a worthy and faithful minister of Christ and the Brethren's Church, he shall be entitled to all the privileges of other ministers of the Church, including the right to sustentation, and the education of his children, but shall not be entitled to

a vote in the Synod in his own right, until his congregation shall have been fully organized and received as a Brethren's Church.

At the present time, there are fourteen missionaries in the field, laboring at the following stations:

Norwich and Greenville, Connecticut, one district and one missionary, commenced in 1857; *Providence*, Rhode Island, one missionary, commenced in 1857; *New York City*, one missionary, commenced in 1851; *Utica*, *Frankfort*, *Ilion*, and *Herkimer*, New York, one district and one missionary, commenced in 1854; *Philadelphia*, Pa., *Palmyra*, *Westfield*, and *Moorestown*, N. J., one district and one missionary, commenced in 1849; *Egg Harbor City*, N. J., one missionary, commenced in 1859; *Wood's Prairie*, Illinois, one missionary, commenced in 1856; *Olney*, Illinois, commenced in 1856 (vacant;) *Green Bay*, *Bay Settlement*, *New Franke*, *Suamico*, and *New Settlement*, Wisconsin, one district and two missionaries, commenced in 1850; *Ephraim*, *Fish Creek*, *Sturgeon Bay*, *Fort Howard*, *Cooperstown*, and *Mishicott*, Wisconsin, one district and one missionary, commenced in 1853; *Lakemills*, *North Salem*, and *Newville*, Wisconsin, one district and one missionary, commenced in 1856; *Ixonia*, Wisconsin, one missionary, commenced in 1857; *Chaska*, *Tabbert*, *Holtmeier*, *Chakopee*, *Henderson*, *Mt. Prairie*, and *Lasour*, Minnesota, one district and one missionary, commenced in 1857; *Coatesville*, Indiana, one missionary, commenced in 1851. Besides these stations, there are several missionaries at the present time serving congregations not in connection with the Moravian Church.

B. The Educational Enterprises.—The Renewed Church of the Brethren began to direct its attention, at an early day, to the cause of education, and its labors, in this respect, have been eminently blessed by God. Thousands not belonging to the communion of the church, have received their education in its Boarding Schools, which, in all the Provinces, enjoy great celebrity and a large patronage.

The educational institutions of the American Province, are the following:

1. *The Moravian College and Theological Seminary.*—This institution was founded in the year 1807, on a small scale, at Nazareth, Pa., but given up again after a time. In 1820, it was re-organized, and in 1838 removed to Bethlehem, where it remained until 1850, when it was once more transferred to Nazareth. The Synod of 1858 entirely remodeled the plan of the institution and enlarged it, ordering its removal to Bethlehem again, where it is now located, in an extensive edifice purchased for the purpose. There are three regular Professors, and the services of ministers at Bethlehem, in case of necessity, are secured as assistants. The institution is endowed to some extent; twenty thousand dollars of the endowment, constituting a special fund, with the interest of which such young men are educated as desire to serve the church, but have not passed through the preparatory

course at Nazareth Hall, and for whose education no other provisions have been made by the church. The expenses of the establishment not covered by the endowment, are paid from the general "Sustentation Fund" (see next chapter) of the Northern District, to which is added an annual contribution from the Southern.

2. *Nazareth Hall*, located at Nazareth, Pa., founded in 1785. This institution is the Classical School, preparatory to the College, and, at the same time, a Boarding School for boys generally, at which upwards of fifteen hundred boys have been educated, from all parts of the United States and the West Indies. The sons of Moravian ministers receive their education here, at the expense of the church, for a period of four years. The teachers, for the most part, are candidates for the ministry, who enter the school after having finished their studies in the Theological Seminary. The average number of boarders annually, is ninety.

3. *Bethlehem Female Seminary*, located at Bethlehem, founded in 1786; a flourishing Boarding School for young ladies, at which more than three thousand five hundred, from every part of the country, have been educated. The average number of boarders annually, is one hundred and seventy.

4. *Linden Hall*, located at Litiz, Pa., founded in 1794; a Boarding School for young ladies, at which nearly two thousand two hundred have been educated. The average number of scholars annually,

including those from the town, is one hundred and forty-five.

5. *Salem Female Academy*, located at Salem, N. C., founded in 1802; a Boarding School for young ladies, celebrated throughout the Southern States, and the largest Boarding School of the church in any part of the Unity. More than three thousand seven hundred young ladies have received their education at this institution, not including those from the town of Salem. The average number of boarders annually is two hundred and twenty. Besides these Boarding Schools, there are several excellent Parochial Schools in the Province, among which that of the church at Bethlehem deserves to be mentioned. It is under the charge of a separate Principal, has eight teachers and about two hundred and twenty pupils.

C. Publcations of the Province.—The Moravian Book Store and Publication office, are located at Bethlehem. Periodical publications are: *The Moravian*, a weekly paper; the *Bruederblatt*, a monthly magazine in the German language; the *Text Book*, a collection of two Scripture passages, one from the Old and the other from the New Testament, each with a corresponding verse from the Hymn Book for every day in the year. This annual, which has appeared without interruption since the year 1731, is published in all the Provinces of the Unity, and prepared by the Unity's Elders' Conference. The most distant mission stations receive it. It appears in the German, English, French, Swedish, Esquimaux, and Negro-

English (used in Surinam, S. A.) languages, and has worked out great good within the church, and among thousands belonging to other communions.

SECTION II.—THE CONTINENTAL PROVINCE.

The churches of the Continental Province, with the exception of three, are *Moravian Settlements*, and still hold to the regulations and have the institutions constituting them such. These regulations are of two kinds,—internal and external.

1. *Internal Regulations.*—Each church is divided, with reference to the station, sex or age of the members, into distinct classes, called *choirs;* namely, those of the married people, the widowers, the widows, the unmarried brethren, the unmarried sisters, the youths, the maidens, and the children. The design of this division is to bring home to every station in life the duties and obligations incumbent upon the same, according to the Holy Scriptures, and thus to facilitate their fulfilment. Each choir is committed to the supervision of one or more elders of its own sex, who care for its spiritual welfare, and watch over the strict observance of the established discipline. These regulations gave to Wesley the idea of the classes, into which the churches of the Methodist denomination are divided. In the British Province, and in a number of the churches of the American, the choirs, to some extent, are kept up. However, in the case of the latter, there are no special super-

intendents, other than the pastors of the churches, who, annually, on the festival days of the choirs, hold services particularly intended for their instruction and edification.

2. *External Regulations.*—The members of the Continental churches live together, in towns and villages, which are exclusively Moravian; or occupy distinct quarters of larger towns. None but members are allowed to hold real estate, although others may lease houses; which is very generally done. In every settlement there is a public inn, and one or more mercantile establishments, or trades, belonging to the church, the profits of which go to its support. This arrangement does not exclude private enterprises and trades, of which there are many. The settlements are governed by a council called the "College of Overseers," elected by the adult male members of the church. At the head of the council stands a deacon, who bears the title of "Warden," and is its executive officer. On business of importance, a general meeting of all the adult male members is convened. The purpose of this exclusive system is to keep out of the congregation, as much as possible, the follies and sins of the world, and to promote sober, righteous and holy living. By the blessing of God, this has been accomplished, in a great degree.

3. *The Institutions.*—The peculiar institutions belonging to a settlement, are the *Brethren's*, *Sisters'*, and *Widows' Houses.* In a Brethren's House, un-

married men live together, and carry on various trades and professions, the profits of which are applied to the support of the establishment, and of the church in general. In a Sisters' House, unmarried women dwell together, and engage in different kinds of female work. In each House there is a common refectory and dormitory; and a prayer-hall, where daily religious services are held. There is nothing monastic in the principles underlying these establishments, or in the regulations by which they are governed. The inmates, who are almost invariably such as have no other homes, stay in the Houses altogether at their own option; are enabled to gain an honest and decent livelihood, which in European countries, with their overstocked population, is a matter of great moment; and enjoy the advantage of particular religious instructions. Nor is this all. These establishments are training-schools, for many of those whom God calls to the work of Foreign Missions. A large number of the Moravian missionaries, and missionaries' wives, now laboring among heathen nations, in different parts of the world, went forth from the Brethren's and Sisters' Houses of the Continental Province. A Widows' House is a home for indigent or other widows; and supplies the inmates with all the comforts which they need, at very moderate charges, enabling even the poorest to live in a respectable manner.

Each House has a spiritual and temporal superintendent. The former cares for the religious welfare of the inmates, and of the whole choir to which they belong; the latter directs the financial concerns. Superintendents of the Sisters' and Widows' Houses are always females.

The spiritual government of a Moravian Continental church, is entrusted to a Board consisting of the ordained ministers, in the service of that church, or of its Boarding Schools, the Warden, and the Superintendents of the several houses described above. This Board is called the *Elders' Conference.* At its head stands the senior pastor of the church.

The churches of the Continental Province are the following:

SAXONY.—*Herrnhut,* in Upper Lusatia, the mother congregation of the Renewed Moravian Church, begun in 1722. It lies on the estate of Berthelsdorf, formerly the property of Count Zinzendorf, now belonging to the Continental Province. About three-quarters of a mile from Herrnhut is *the village of Berthelsdorf,* where the Unity's Elders' Conference has its seat. The members, with their families, live partly in the castle, once the residence of Zinzendorf, and partly in two large mansions that have been erected near it. In the castle is the Conference-Room, where the Board meets, and aside of it a prayer-hall, in which the members and their families gather for daily worship. *Kleinwelke,* begun in 1751, in Upper Lusatia. Here the schools for the education of the children of the missionaries of the church are located.

PRUSSIA.—*Niesky*, in Upper Lusatia, begun in 1742. This is the seat of the College of the Continental Province. *Gnadau*, in the county of Barby, begun in 1747. *Gnadenfrei*, in the principality of Schweidnitz, begun in 1743. *Gnadenberg*, in the principality of Jauer, begun in 1743. *Neusalz*, in the principality of Glogau, begun in 1744. This settlement constitutes a distinct quarter of the town of Neusalz, on the Oder; the members living together in that quarter, as in other settlements. *Gnadenfeld*, in the principality of Oppeln, begun in 1780. This is the seat of the Continental Theological Seminary. All these churches, with the exception of Niesky, are in the Province of Silesia. *Neuwied*, on the Rhine, begun in 1750. The settlement comprises a distinct quarter of the town, as at Neusalz. *Berlin*, begun in 1744. This is not a settlement, but an ordinary city congregation. *Rixdorf*, begun in 1756, three miles from Berlin. A country congregation, and no settlement.

HANOVER.—*Norden*, in East Friesland, begun in 1743. This is a small country congregation.

GRAND DUCHY OF BADEN.—*Koenigsfeld*, begun in 1807.

DUCHY OF SAXE-GOTHA.—*Neudientendorf*, near Erfurt, begun in 1753.

PRINCIPALITY OF REUSS-SCHLEITZ.—*Ebersdorf*, begun in 1746.

DENMARK.—*Christiansfeld*, in the duchy of Sleswick, begun in 1772.

HOLLAND.—*Zeist*, near Utrecht, begun in 1746.

Harlem, new church built in 1841. A city congregation.

RUSSIA.—*Sarepta*, on the Wolga, near Zarizyn, begun in 1765.

Enterprises of the Continental Province.

A. THE DIASPORA.—This is one of the most interesting works of which modern church-history knows. It is a mission among the state churches of the Continent of Europe, having their evangelization for its object, without thereby severing the ecclesiastical connection of their members. About one hundred and twenty missionaries are engaged in this work, at present. Each missionary has a district, in which he labors. It is his duty to visit from house to house, and to hold meetings for prayer and exhortation, at stated times. The persons visited are divided into two classes. The first comprises "the Brethren and Sisters of the Diaspora," in general; that is, such as receive the visits of the missionary and attend his ordinary meetings. The second comprehends the "Societies of the Brethren." These consist of persons who desire to maintain a closer fellowship with the Moravian Church, and are formed into Societies, governed by certain rules, and presided over by the missionary. For the members of these Societies all the religious services peculiar to the Moravian Church on the Continent, are held; but the missionary never administers the sacraments. These the members of the Societies receive in the state churches, to which they continue to belong; and in which they also attend on the regular ministrations of the Word. In this manner, Spener's idea of little churches within the church, has been very extensively realized.

The name given to this circle of awakened souls, scattered throughout the Protestant Churches of Europe, is the "*Diaspora of the Brethren's Church.*" It came into use in the year 1750, and is taken from 1 Pet. i. 1, according to the original Greek: "Peter, an apostle of Jesus Christ, to the elect strangers of the *Diaspora* of Pontus," &c., that is, "living scattered throughout Pontus," &c.

The mode of conducting the work is the same, as to principles, in all the countries of Europe to which it has extended, but varies in its details according to the ecclesiastical peculiarities of the state in which it is going on. In some cases, the missionary resides permanently in his district; in others he visits there statedly, from neighboring Moravian churches. Many districts have regular chapels, or prayer-halls, for religious services; in others, these are held in private houses. The enterprise is supported chiefly by the contributions of the Society-members themselves, aided by grants made from the funds of the Continental Province.

At the present time, the Diaspora embraces the following provinces of various countries on the Continent:

I. Germany.—*Upper Lusatia*, *Lower Lusatia*,

Silesia, Upper Silesia, Berlin and Province Brandenburg, Pommerania, Newmark, Koenigsberg and Province Prussia, Province Saxony, Thuringia, Kingdom of Saxony, Brunswick, Bremen, Oldenburg, East Friesland, Upper Rhine, Lower Rhine, Middle Rhine, Wurtemberg.

II. SWITZERLAND AND FRANCE.—*Cantons Basle, Bern, Zurich, French Switzerland, Alsace, South France.*

III. DENMARK, NORWAY, AND SWEDEN.—*Altona and Hamburg, Copenhagen and region about, Jutland, Sleswick and Holstein, Christiania and region about, Drontheim and region about, Stockholm and region about, Gothenburg and region about.*

IV. RUSSIAN EMPIRE.—*Livonia, Esthonia, part of Poland, and St. Petersburg.*

The work in Russia is very extensive, particularly in Livonia and Esthonia, where there are two hundred and sixty-two chapels. The whole number of souls belonging to the Diaspora, is about eighty thousand.

B. HOME MISSION.—Distinct from the Diaspora, are various smaller enterprises, among the destitute peasantry, carried on by private Associations, in the immediate neighborhood of some of the Continental churches. The *Children's Home and Spinning School,* near Herrnhut, deserve to be particularly mentioned.

C. EDUCATIONAL ENTERPRISES.—These are numerous and in a flourishing condition.

1. *The Theological Seminary*, located at Gnadenfeld, in Silesia, founded in 1754, an excellent institution, with three Professors.

2. *The College*, called *Paedagogium*, located at Niesky, in Prussia, founded in 1754. Average number of students, fifty; of Professors, nine.

3. *Boarding Schools for Boys and Girls*, at which a large number of pupils not belonging to the church are educated. The number of these schools in this Province amounts to twenty-five, as follows: at *Christiansfeld*, two, (one for boys, and the other for girls;) at *Ebersdorf*, two; at *Gnadau* and *Gnadenberg*, each two; at *Gnadenfrei*, one for girls; at *Kleinwelke*, two, for the children of the missionaries; at *Koenigsfeld*, two; at *Neudientendorf*, two; at *Neusalz*, one for girls; at *Neuwied*, two; at *Niesky*, one for boys; at *Zeist*, two. Besides these institutions, located in the midst of regular settlements, this Province has the following: At *Lindheim*, in Livonia, a school for girls; at *Lausanne*, on Lake Geneva, in Switzerland, an excellent school for boys; at *Montauban*, in France, a school for girls; and at *Montmirail*, in the Canton of Neuchaftel, Switzerland, a celebrated Seminary for young ladies, a kind of Normal Boarding School, where many of the teachers employed in the other schools of the church are educated.

D. PUBLICATIONS.—The Church Book Store of this Province is located at Gnadau, in Prussia. The following are the periodical publications:

1. *The Text Book*, an annual, as in the American Province.

2. The *Missionsblatt*, a monthly missionary magazine.

3. *Nachrichten aus der Bruedergemeine*, a monthly magazine, containing discourses, sermons, memoirs, missionary accounts, &c.

4 *Nachrichten aus der Bruedergemeine, als Manuscript gedruckt*, a similar magazine, giving accounts particularly from the Diaspora.

5. *Nachrichten aus der U. A. C.*, a short report issued by the Unity's Elders' Conference, and containing the latest intelligence from all parts of the Unitas Fratrum. Published monthly.

E. THE MINISTERS' CONFERENCE AT HERRNHUT.—This may very properly be classed among the enterprises of the church on the Continent. In the year 1754, a number of ministers of the state church residing in the neighborhood of Herrnhut, met at Berthelsdorf, with several Moravian ministers, for the purpose of conversing on subjects connected with their calling, consulting together on the furtherance of the work of God, and entering into a fraternal union. Since that time, "the Ministers' Conference of Herrnhut," has continued to assemble annually, and greatly extended the sphere of its operations. Between sixty and seventy ministers of the state church attend it in person, and there are numerous corresponding members in different parts of Germany, Switzerland, France, Holland, England, Denmark, Norway, Sweden, and the United States.

SECTION III.—THE BRITISH PROVINCE.

Among the churches of the British Province, there are four settlements like those on the Continent, the rest are all ordinary churches. The following is the list:

In ENGLAND, *London* and *Chelsea* begun in 1738; *Ockbrook*, in Derbyshire, begun in 1740; a Moravian settlement, the seat of the British Provincial Board; *Fulneck* and *Horton* begun in 1742, the former a Moravian settlement, the latter an affiliated congregation in the neighborhood; *Wyke* begun in 1742; *Mirfield* begun in 1742; *Gomersal* begun in 1742; *Baildon* begun in 1780. All these are in Yorkshire. *Fairfield*, in Lancashire, begun in 1768, a Moravian settlement; *Salem*, in Lancashire, begun in 1825; *Leominster*, in Herefordshire, begun in 1755; *Woodford*, in Northampton, begun in 1792; *Bedford*, in Bedfordshire, begun in 1742; *Kimbolton*, in Huntingdonshire, begun in 1823; *Risely*, in Bedfordshire, begun in 1742; *Pertenhall*, in Bedfordshire, begun in 1823; *Bristol*, in Gloucestershire, begun in 1748; *Kingswood*, in Gloucestershire, begun in 1740; *Brockweir*, in Monmouthshire, begun in 1833; *Bath*, in Somersetshire, begun in 1760; *Boltonsborough*, in Somersetshire, begun in 1852; *Tytherton*, in Wiltshire, begun in 1742; *Malmesbury*, in Wiltshire, begun in 1742; *Devonport*, in Devonshire, begun in 1769; and *Dukinfield*.

In WALES, *Haverfordwest*, with *Purdine* and *Portfield*, begun in 1753.

In SCOTLAND, *Ayr*, in Ayrshire, begun in 1768.

In IRELAND, *Dublin* begun in 1746; *Gracehill*, Antrim County, a Moravian settlement, begun in 1751; *Ballinderry*, in Antrim County, begun in 1751; *Gracefield*, in Londonderry County, begun in 1751; *Kilwarlin*, in Down County, begun in 1751; *Kilkeel*, in Down County, begun in 1752; *Cootehill*, in Cavan County, begun in 1754.

Enterprises of the British Province.

A. EDUCATIONAL ENTERPRISES.—This Province has no Theological Seminary or College of its own. Young men studying for the ministry are generally educated in the institutions of the church on the Continent. There are, however, a number of Boarding Schools, namely: At *Bedford*, one for girls; at *Dukinfield*, one for girls; at *Fairfield*, two, (one for boys, the other for girls;) at *Fulneck*, two; at *Ockbrook*, two; at *Gracehill*, two; at *Gomersal*, one for girls; at *Mirfield*, one for boys; at *Tytherton* and *Wyke*, each, one for girls; fifteen in all.

B. HOME MISSION.—This is a cause carried on by means of Scripture readers in Ireland, who visit the cottages of the poor, reading and explaining to them the word of God. The Foreign Mission work engages the particular attention of the British Province, which takes the lead in promoting this cause.

C. Publications.—The Church Book Store is located in London. Periodical publications are the following: *The Text Book*, as in the other Provinces; the *Periodical Accounts*, a quarterly magazine, devoted to the interests of the Foreign Mission work, and established in 1790; the *Fraternal Record*, a monthly miscellany not published by the church, but a private enterprise.

Having given an account of the three Provinces of the Moravian Brethren's Unity, as they at present appear, and of the enterprises carried on by each, we proceed to the great work which engages the chief attention of the church, and in which all the Provinces unitedly take part. It is the cause of Foreign Missions.

SECTION IV.—THE FOREIGN MISSION WORK OF THE MORAVIAN CHURCH.

The Foreign Mission work was begun in the year 1732, ten years after the erection of the first house at Herrnhut, when this congregation, numbering about six hundred souls, constituted the only Moravian church in existence. Leonard Dober and David Nitschmann, the latter afterwards the first Bishop of the Renewed Church, were the pioneers, and proceeded to the island of St. Thomas, where a mission was established among the negro slaves. Since that time, although not all the enterprises which were undertaken proved successful, the cause has prospered beyond the most sanguine hopes of the early

Brethren. The missionary spirit, in the first stage of its development, manifested itself particularly among the immigrants from Moravia. It was, therefore, the life of the Ancient Unitas, a life which Rome could not quench, that gave the impulse to the great work in which all evangelical churches are now actively engaged, and extended the principles of the Reformers before the Reformation, to countries whose existence was unknown when Hus preached the gospel in Bohemia, and Gregory laid the foundations of the Brethren's Church.

Up to the year 1852, the church had sent out one thousand nine hundred aud forty-seven missionaries, male and female. Taking the annual average of those who entered the service since then to have been twenty, the whole number of missionaries, male and female, who went forth from the Moravian Church in the one hundred and twenty-seven years of the existence of the Foreign Mission enterprise, amounts to *two thousand and eighty-seven.*

Since the commencement of the work, unsuccessful attempts to establish Missions, have been made in the following countries: *Lapland*, among the *Samoyedes*, *Algiers*, *Ceylon*, *China*, *Persia*, *East Indies*, *Caucasus*, and *Demarara.* In the following countries Missions were established, but suspended again: *Guinea*, among the *Calmucks*, *Abyssinia*, and *Tranquebar.*

The present extent of the Foreign Mission field, which is generally divided into Provinces, is the following:

First Province, *Greenland*, four stations: New Herrnhut, Lichtenfels, Lichtenau, and Fredericksthal.

Second Province, *Labrador*, four stations: Nain, Hopedale, Okak, and Hebron.

Third Province, *North America*, four stations: New Fairfield, in Canada West, among Delaware Indians; Westfield, in Kansas, among Delaware Indians; New Spring Place, and Canaan, among the Cherokees, in the Cherokee country.

Fourth Province, *Central America*, three stations: Bluefields, Magdala, and Rama Key, among the Mosquito Indians and the negroes of the Mosquito Coast.

Fifth Province, *Danish West Indies*, eight stations: New Herrnhut, Nisky, Town of St. Thomas, in St. Thomas; Friedensthal, Friedensberg, and Friedensfeld, in St. Croix; Bethany and Emmaus, in St. Jan.

Sixth Province, *Jamaica*, thirteen stations: Fairfield, New Eden, Irwin Hill, New Carmel, New Bethlehem, New Fulneck, New Nazareth, Beaufort, New Hope, Lititz, Bethany, Bethabara, Springfield.

Seventh Province, *Antigua*, seven stations: St. Johns, Gracehill, Gracebay, Cedar Hall, Newfield, Lebanon, Gracefield.

Eighth Province, *St. Kitts*, four stations: Basseterre, Bethesda, Estridge, Bethel.

Ninth Province, *Barbadoes*, four stations: Sharon, Bridgetown, Mount Tabor, Clifton Hill.

Tenth Province, *Tobago*, two stations: Montgomery, Moriah.

ELEVENTH PROVINCE, *Surinam, in South America*, ten stations: Paramaribo, District of the Para, Rust-en-Werk, Liliendal, Annaszorg, Charlottenburg, Catharine Sophia, Herrendyk, Salem, New Bambey.

TWELFTH PROVINCE, *South Africa*, eight stations: Genadendal, Mamre, Robben Island, Elim, Enon, Clarkson, Shiloh, Goshen.

THIRTEENTH PROVINCE, *Thibet, in Asia*, one station: Kyelang.

FOURTEENTH PROVINCE, *Australia*, one station, on the Wimmera river.

There are fourteen Provinces, and seventy-three regular stations.* The number of missionaries, male and female, at present in the field, is *three hundred and five;* the total number of converts under instruction, *seventy-four thousand five hundred and thirty-eight.* The converts belong to the following races:—Greenlanders, Esquimaux, Indians, Negroes, Kaffres, Hottentots, Fingoos, and Tambookies; and besides, the gospel is preached to Thibetans and Papuans, but none of these latter races have as yet been brought to a knowledge of the Truth.

In all the Mission Provinces, particular attention is paid to the mental and spiritual education of the children, and numerous day and Sunday-schools have been organized. The school system is particularly developed in the British West Indies. In Jamaica, more than three thousand children are educated in the Mission Schools.

* Merely the regular stations are counted. There are many out-stations, or preaching-places.

Training or Normal Schools have been established in the following Provinces, for the education of native assistants: *South Africa*, school organized in 1838; *Jamaica*, school organized in 1842; *Antigua*, school organized in 1847, a second institution in the same island for native female assistants; *Greenland*, school organized in 1850; *Surinam*, school organized in 1851; six training institutions in all.

In carrying on the mission work, it has always been a fundamental principle of the church, to manifest—in the language of the "Synodal Results"—"less solicitude to bring a great number of persons to a profession of the Christian faith, than, by means of the gospel preached with demonstration of the Spirit and of power, 'to turn souls from darkness unto light, from the power of Satan unto God.' For this purpose, the preaching of the gospel must be accompanied by *the special care of individual souls;* periodical conversations of the missionaries with the members of their congregations, according to their several classes, and visits to the houses and to the beds of the sick and dying, are deemed of the utmost importance." (Synodal Results, 1858, § 102.) This principle is faithfully observed in all the Mission Provinces. In order to facilitate its application, the converts are divided into the following classes: 1. *New People*, the lowest class, comprising those who have applied to the missionaries for instruction. These are taught the rudiments of the Christian religion. 2. *Candidates for Baptism*, a higher class, to which such from the former are promoted, as receive instruction preparatory to their baptism. 3. *Baptized Adults*, a still higher class, to which those belong who have been baptized. 4. *Communicants*, the highest class, to which those of the former are promoted who have been confirmed and admitted to the Lord's Supper. There are besides two other classes: *Baptized Children*—the children of parents in fellowship with the church. *Excluded*—those under church discipline, who receive particular attention from the missionaries.

The manner in which the mission work of the Moravian Church is supported, constitutes a subject of interest and importance. In the fiscal year 1857, the whole amount required for this purpose was not quite 250,000 German (Rix) dollars, or about $182,926, U. S. currency. The principal items of expense are: the maintenance of the missionaries, and their journeys; the erection of church edifices, school and mission houses; the support of the Normal and Day Schools; pensions to retired missionaries and widows of missionaries; the education of the children of missionaries; salaries of the members of the Board, agents, &c. The missionaries themselves receive no fixed salary, while in the service, but a decent and comfortable support; enjoying, besides, the advantages just enumerated, namely, the right to have their children educated, at the expense of the church, and a pension when they leave the field, on account of sickness or old age. If a missionary dies, his widow is pensioned.

The sources of revenue upon which the church depends for prosecuting the work, are the following:

1. Annual contributions from the members in the three Provinces of the Unity; and from other friends of the cause, by whom a large amount is given, especially in England.

2. Interest received from several funded legacies, which have been left with the proviso that the capital shall not be touched.

3. Other legacies.

4. Contributions and donations of Missionary Associations, established in the three Provinces of the Unity. This is a very important source of income, and without it, the work could not be carried on. In the American Province, there are Societies of this kind in a number of the churches. The principal one is *The Society of the United Brethren for Propagating the Gospel among the Heathen*, whose board has its seat at Bethlehem. This Association was incorporated in 1788. All bishops, presbyters, and deacons of the Moravian Church, in the United States, are, ex officio, members of it; the other members are elected. It holds a funded capital, and its annual contribution to the mission treasury is between $9,000 and $10,000. A similar Society exists at Salem, N. C. *Female Missionary Societies* have been established at Bethlehem, Nazareth, Litiz, &c.; *Young Men's Missionary Societies* at Bethlehem, Litiz, Salem, &c. In Ohio there is an efficient Association, composed of members from the four churches of Tuscarawas County. The most active and im-

portant Missionary Societies, however, are found in the British Province, the two principal ones being the following: *The Brethren's Society for the Furtherance of the Gospel among the Heathen*, established in 1741; and *The London Association in Aid of the Missions of the United Brethren*, founded in 1817. The former devotes its strength particularly to the furtherance of the mission in Labrador, bearing nearly the entire burden of this enterprise. This Society owns a missionary ship, called "The Harmony," which is annually sent out to the coast of Labrador, in order to supply the missionaries with the necessaries of life.* The other Society is composed chiefly of Christians not in church-fellowship with the Moravian Brethren, but desirous to aid in promoting their missions. Its average annual contributions amount to £5,000. In the Continental Province there are also a number of Associations; and in several Mission Provinces the same mode of aiding the cause has been successfully tried.

5. The last and one of the principal sources of revenue, are the missions themselves, which contribute largely to their own support, and some of them are entirely self-supporting. Were it not for this

* The first vessel owned by the society was the *Amity*, which was sent on her first voyage in 1771. Since that time eight vessels have been successively employed in the service of the mission. The present *Harmony* was built in 1831, and is a brig of 230 tons register. During the whole period of eighty seven annual voyages, no accident has ever befallen the missionary ship, nor has the communication between the missionaries and the Brethren in Europe been in a single instance interrupted.

circumstance, the extensive work which is going on in foreign countries would have to be curtailed at once. In the year 1857 about $95,338 were raised by the missions; partly by the voluntary contributions of the converts, especially in the West Indies; and partly from the profits of mercantile concerns and trades, carried on in some of the Mission Provinces, especially Surinam and South Africa. Many missionaries, like the tent-maker Paul, who was an apostle of the Lord Jesus Christ, are not ashamed to aid the cause by the labor of their hands.

However, numerous as the sources of revenue are, and large as is the amount coming from the missions themselves, the entire work remains pre-eminently one of *faith*. Since the commencement of the enterprise, many a year was closed with a heavy debt resting upon the church, owing to unforeseen expenses, or to the failure of income. Yet up to the present time, by the blessing of God, the greatest financial difficulties have always been overcome, and the work has been continued without interruption. The last General Synod reiterated the principle that the foreign missions of the church constitute a cause for the support of which the faith of the whole Unity is pledged.

The management and superintendence of the mission work are entrusted to a Board of four members, forming one of the Committees, or Departments of the Unity's Elders' Conference, (see next chapter,) and called "The Mission Department."

CHAPTER III.

THE CONSTITUTION.

INTRODUCTION.

The Moravian Church, as was stated in the preceding chapter, is divided into three Provinces. These constitute independent organizations in so far as their own local affairs are concerned, but are confederated as one church, or Unity, in respect to certain principles of doctrine and practice, and the work of foreign missions. Hence there must be a general government for the united church, and separate governments for the several provinces. The relation in which the latter stand to the former is similar to that existing between the individual commonwealths of the United States and the federal government. Each commonwealth has a legislative and an executive power of its own; and, at the same time, there is a Congress of the United States, and an executive for the whole Union. So in the Moravian Church. There is a legislative and executive body in each Province; and a General Synod, and General Executive Board for the whole Unity. The government is vested in the Synods, which appoint the Executive Boards.

From this it appears that the Constitution of the Church may be classified as follows: 1. The general Constitution of the Unity; 2. The particular Constitutions of the American, Continental, and British Provinces.

SECTION I.—GENERAL CONSTITUTION OF THE UNITY.

THE GENERAL SYNOD.

Purpose of the Synod.

The bishops, ministers and delegates assembled at a General Synod, shall represent the Brethren's Unity, and act in its name. To the General Synod shall, therefore, belong all legislation in reference to the general concerns of the Unity; it shall carefully examine, correct and lay down anew the principles upon which the Unity is based; it shall, in view of these principles, investigate the state and condition of the Unity as a whole, and of its parts, and ascertain in how far these principles have been observed in the Provinces; it shall make such arrangements, and adopt such resolutions, as the well-being of the Unity may demand; and it shall be the occasion for a mutual interchange of ideas and experiences, on the part of the representatives of the several Provinces, for the furthering of God's work in them, and in the Unity at large.

Powers of the General Synod.

The General Synod shall have power:

a. To determine all points or questions of doctrine.

b. To establish the fundamental rules of the liturgy of the church.

c. To prescribe the fundamental principles of discipline.

d. To specify the qualifications of membership in the Moravian Brethren's Church.

e. To appoint or provide for the appointment of bishops.

f. To regulate and direct all matters pertaining to the foreign missions.

g. To control such educational institutions as belong to the whole Unity.

h. To direct and superintend all financial affairs of the Unity.

i. To elect the Unity's Elders' Conference and prescribe the mode of filling vacancies in the same.

j. To regulate the formation and times of meeting of the General Synod, and establish the basis of representation in the same.

k. To direct all matters which belong to the general constitution of the Brethren's Unity, and its church regulations.

Members of the General Synod.

The following shall be members of the General Synod:

a. The members of the existing Unity's Elders' Conference.

b. The bishops of the Moravian United Brethren's Church.

c. One member of each Provincial Elders' Conference, provided no member of said Conference attends the Synod in another capacity.

d. The secretary of the Unity, in England.

e. The administrators of the church property in Pennsylvania and North Carolina, U. S.

f. The cashier of the Unity's funds.

g. The treasurer of the foreign missions.

h. The archivist of the Unity.

i. Nine elected delegates from the American Province. (Seven from Northern, and two from the Southern District.)

j. Nine elected delegates from the Continental Province.

k. Nine elected delegates from the British Province.

l. Not less than five missionaries, from the several foreign mission fields, to be designated by the Unity's Elders' Conference, after having received confidential votes from the individual missionaries.

m. Such brethren as are conversant with subjects that may come up for deliberation, and whose presence the Unity's Elders' Conference may deem particularly important, shall be advisory members, but without a vote.

Election of Delegates to the General Synod.

Delegates to the General Synod, from the several Provinces, shall be elected by the Provincial Synod of each Province. All brethren shall be eligible who have been members of the church for two years, who are communicants, and more than twenty-four years of age.

For each delegate, an alternate may be elected.

The manner of electing the delegates shall be left to the Provincial Synod of each Province to determine.

Organization of the General Synod.

The General Synod shall be opened by the President of the existing Unity's Elders' Conference, but shall organize by electing its own officers.

All members of the Synod shall have an equal right to vote.

In cases of great importance, Synod may agree to leave the final decision to the Lord, by the lot; but there must be, so far as possible, unanimity of sentiment in reference to the use of the lot at such times.

In case two Provinces should unite in an attempt to force upon the third, by a majority of votes, a change in the existing general rules of the Unity, in spite of the protestations of the delegates of that Province, two-thirds of its delegates have power to unite in a veto, and thereby annul any resolution of this kind adopted by the majority, so far as its observance in the whole Unity is concerned. None but the elected delegates of a Province shall take part in this vote.

Expenses of the General Synod.

The journeys and maintenance of the members of the General Synod, shall be defrayed from the *Synodical Fund* created by the Synod of 1857, and belonging to the whole Unity. After each Synod, the accounts of this fund shall be closed, and a statement of its receipts and disbursements sent to the churches of the several Provinces.

THE UNITY'S ELDERS' CONFERENCE.

Purpose of the Unity's Elders' Conference.

The General Synod shall elect an Executive Board of twelve members, called *The Unity's Elders' Conference*, to which shall be committed the oversight and direction of the Unity, from one Synod to another, in all things appertaining to the powers of the General Synod. This Board shall act in the name and by the authority of the General Synod, and shall be responsible to said Synod; but all officers or other boards appointed by the General Synod, or by the Unity's Elders' Conference, shall be responsible to it. The Unity's Elders' Conference shall receive from the Synod a power of attorney, by which it shall be accredited as the Directing Board of the Brethren's Unity.

Powers of the Unity's Elders' Conference.

The Unity's Elders' Conference shall have power:

a. To direct and administer all the general affairs of the Unity, in accordance with the principles and rules laid down by the General Synod.

b. By keeping up a regular correspondence with the Provincial Boards, which are to submit to it copies of their minutes and copies of the journals of the Provincial Synods; to see that the enactments of the General Synod are faithfully executed in the whole Unity.

c. To convene the General Synod in cases of emergency.

d. In the event of an extraordinary emergency, to abrogate a rule of the General Synod for the time being; said abrogation, however, to be made the subject of a special report to the next General Synod, setting forth the reasons which induced it.

e. To send one or more of its members on official visits to the Provinces and the Foreign Mission fields; said visits to take place, as far as possible, on the occasion of Provincial Synods.

Organization of the Unity's Elders' Conference.

The Unity's Elders' Conference shall organize by the election of its own officers, consisting of a President and Vice-President, and appoint its Recording Secretaries, who shall not be members of the Board.

The Unity's Elders' Conference shall be divided into three departments:

1. *The Elders' and Education Department,* having particular superintendence over the spiritual state of the Unity, and over the Unity's educational institutions.

2. *The Warden's Department,* to which the financial concerns of the Unity shall be committed.

3. *The Mission Department,* having charge of the Foreign Mission work.

Each department shall consist of four members.

Election of the Unity's Elders' Conference.

As soon as the General Synod has been fully organized, the Unity's Elders' Conference shall resign in a body. Before the Synod adjourns, a new Board shall be elected, according to the following rules:

a. Members of the late Board shall be re-eligible.

b. A majority of votes shall be necessary for an election.

c. Each Synod shall decide in how far and in what manner the lot shall be used, for the purpose of confirming the election.

Vacancies in the Unity's Elders' Conference.

In case a vacancy occurs in the Unity's Elder's Conference in the interval between one General Synod and the next, the Unity's Elders' Conference shall issue a circular, notifying the Provinces of the same, and calling upon them for their votes. Said votes shall be regarded in the light of *proposals;* the election itself shall belong to the Board, and take place in full session.

The votes shall be distributed as follows:

1. Each department of the Unity's Elders' Conference shall have two votes.

2. The Continental Province shall have sixteen votes.

3. The British Province shall have twelve votes.

4. The American Province shall have eleven votes: eight for the Northern, and three for the Southern District.

When the votes have all been returned to the Unity's Elders' Conference,—and each ticket should contain the names of three brethren,—this Board shall proceed to the election, guided by the votes received, and subject to the confirmation of the Lord, by the use of the lot. The name of no brother having less than one-third of all the votes returned shall be submitted to the lot.

A protocol of the election shall be drawn up and signed by all the members of the Board; the substance of which shall be communicated to the Provinces.

The Unity's Elders' Conference shall not create vacancies by appointing one or more of its members to other offices in the church.

Finances of the Unity.

The Unity, as such, shall hold in common, three funds:

1. The Foreign Mission Fund; by which are meant the receipts for the Foreign Missions from societies, churches, and individuals, together with the principal and interest of all funded capitals held and administered by the Mission Board.

2. The Synodical Fund, created by the Synod of 1857, from which the expenses of the General Synod shall be defrayed.

3. The Fund for the maintenance of the Unity's Elders' Conference, from which fund those members of this body shall be salaried who are not supported by the Foreign Mission Fund, or by the Continental Province.*

SECTION II.—CONSTITUTIONS OF THE THREE PROVINCES.—GENERAL PRINCIPLES.

The government of the Provinces, so far as all provincial matters are concerned, shall be vested in their respective Provincial Synods. To these shall belong the supreme direction of provincial concerns, and the power to legislate on them. But no resolutions shall be adopted conflicting

* The Unity's Elders' Conference being, for the present, the Provincial Conference of the Continental Province, some of the members are maintained by that Province.

with the principles and rules of the Unity as established by the General Synod.

The Executive Boards for the management of the provincial affairs of the Provinces, shall be the Provincial Elders' Conferences, which shall be responsible to the Provincial Synods. Said Conferences shall, therefore, on the one hand, in connection with the Unity's Elders' Conference, see that the resolutions of the General Synod are faithfully carried out in the Provinces, and on the other, independently of the Unity's Elders' Conference, (unless a Provincial Synod has otherwise ordered,) act as the Executive Boards of the Provincial Synods by which they are elected.

A. THE CONSTITUTION OF THE NORTHERN DISTRICT OF THE AMERICAN PROVINCE.

THE PROVINCIAL SYNOD.

Powers of the Provincial Synod.

The Synod of the Northern District of the American Province shall have power:

a. To fix the time and place of meeting for the next Provincial Synod, but in case of emergency, the Provincial Elders' Conference may convene the Synod at an earlier day.

b. To determine from time to time the number of delegates each church shall be entitled to send to such Synod, and the manner of their election.

c. To elect the delegates which the Province may be entitled to send to the General Synod.

d. To elect an Executive Committee, to be called the Provincial Elders' Conference, to consist of such number of members as the Provincial Synod may from time to time determine, to be chosen from among the ordained ministers of the church.

e. To elect the President of the College and Theological Seminary.

f. To examine and direct all financial matters of the Province, and prescribe rules for their management.

g. To oversee and direct all the educational concerns of the Province.

h. To regulate the organization of churches, and direct Home Missions in the Province.

i. To direct and control all church publications in the Province, subject to the established doctrine and liturgy.

j. To prescribe the mode of nominating the Bishops.

k. To hear and redress complaints and grievances, and generally to direct all matters which belong to the government of the church in the Province, and to adopt rules and regulations concerning the same not inconsistent with the powers of the General Synod.

Organization of the Synod.

The Provincial Synod shall be opened by the President of the Provincial Elders' Conference, but shall organize by electing its own officers; the President to be chosen from among the Bishops of the Province.

Members of the Synod.

The following shall be members of the Provincial Synod of the Northern district of the American Province:

a. The members of the existing Provincial Elders' Conference.

b. All Bishops of the Moravian Church residing in the Province, whether in actual service or not.

c. All ordained ministers of the church in the Province who are in actual service as pastors, or in the various educational institutions.

d. The delegates from the different churches of the Province.

e. The members of the Unity's Elders' Conference or their delegates, the delegates of the several Provinces of the Unity, the financial agent of the Unity's Elders' Conference in the Province, the delegates of Synods of other denominations with which the Provincial Synod stands in correspondence, and such other brethren as the Provincial Synod may determine upon, shall be entitled to seats as advisory members, but without a vote.

THE PROVINCIAL ELDERS' CONFERENCE.

Powers of the Provincial Elders' Conference.

The Provincial Elders' Conference of this Province shall have power:

a. To appoint one of their number to act as President.

b. To see that the enactments of General Synods are faithfully executed in the Province.

c. To appoint and control all ministers and other servants of the Province; but the Synod shall have the right to elect the President of the College and Theological Seminary.

d. In cases of emergency, to convene the Provincial Synod.

e. To administer the government of the church in the Province generally, under such rules and regulations as shall be adopted from time to time by the Provincial Synod.

Vacancies in the Provincial Elders' Conference.

Vacancies occurring in the Provincial Elders' Conference during the recess of the Synod, shall be filled as follows: The Provincial Elders' Conference shall issue its circular to the different congregations and other persons interested, giving them notice of such vacancy, and directing them to vote for a brother among the ministry to fill the same. In the election, every person who is ex-officio entitled to a seat and vote in the Provincial Synod shall have one vote, and each congregation shall be entitled to as many votes as such congregation was entitled to send delegates to the Provincial Synod last held, to be given by them as they may see proper. The votes, as given, shall be sealed up and sent to the Provincial Elders' Conference, who shall receive them, but break no seal until all the votes have been received and their own vote or votes added thereto. The votes shall then be opened and counted in the presence of not less than two other brethren, and if any brother shall have a majority of all the votes given, he shall be considered elected. Should no brother have a majority of all the votes given, the Provincial Elders' Conference shall issue another circular as before, giving the names of the three brethren who received the highest number of votes. The ministers of congregations and all others entitled to vote, shall then again vote in a manner above described, but shall be confined in their votes to the three brethren named. When the votes have again been returned to the Provincial Elders' Conference, as above stated, and after their vote has been added, they shall open and count the votes in the presence of witnesses as before, and the brother having the highest number of votes, shall be considered elected. After each election, the Provincial Elders' Conference shall publish a full account thereof.

Finances of the Province.

From the *Sustentation Fund** shall be paid:

* A brief explanatory statement in reference to this Fund is here inserted. Formerly, the American Province North held no

a. The salaries of the members of the Provincial Elders' Conference, and other expenses incidental to their office.

b. The pensions of superannuated ministers, and of widows of ministers.

---

funded property. The yearly expenditures were defrayed by contributions from the more wealthy churches, by appropriations from the annual profits of the Church Boarding Schools, if such profits accrued, and from occasional legacies. Whenever, at the close of a financial year, a deficit occurred, the Province had to look to the funds of the Unity for aid. But in the course of the last ten years, agreements were entered into between the authorities of the Province on the one hand, and several of the more wealthy churches of the same on the other; in consequence of which agreements, the latter, in lieu of annual contributions, ceded a considerable portion of their property to the Province. In this way certain funds were created, the yearly interest of which is appropriated to defray the current expenditures of the church in the Province. At the General Synod of 1857, a division of the funds held by the Unity in general, was resolved on, and has since then been carried out. The portion paid to the American Province North, amounts to about $25,000; of which $20,000, according to the enactment of the Provincial Synod of 1858, have been set apart as a special endowment of the Moravian College. Consequently, the interest accruing from these several funds, the yearly surpluses, if any, of the Boarding Schools belonging to the church, an annual contribution from the American Province South, and the annual amount of $1,200 bequeathed to the church for educational purposes, constitute the yearly income of the American Province North. The property obtained in the manner now stated and belonging to the church of this Province, is commonly called the "Sustentation Fund." This Fund is managed by the Provincial Elders' Conference, which is a body corporate in law; having been incorporated in the year 1851, by the Legislature of the State of Pennsylvania, under the style and title of "The Board of Elders of the Northern Diocese of the church of the United Brethren in the United States of America." An *c*. The expenses incurred by the education of the children of the ministers, to which education, in the institutions of the church, such children shall be entitled for a period of four years.

d. The expenses connected with the Moravian College and Theological Seminary, over and above the income from the endowment fund.

e. The deficit, if any, incurred by the publications of the church.

f. In case of necessity, contributions to ministers in destitute churches, and, in cases of emergency, to such churches themselves.

g. An annual appropriation of $500 to the Home Mission cause of the Northern District.

h. The expenses incurred by the holding of Provincial Synods, in so far as said expenses are not covered by collections in the churches for this purpose.

PRESENT BY-LAWS TO THE CONSTITUTION OF THE NORTHERN DISTRICT OF THE AMERICAN PROVINCE.

I. *Provincial Synod.*—The Provincial Synod shall be convened once in every three years, and all Officers and Boards appointed by the Synod, shall report to the same; the reading of which reports shall be the first business in order after the organization of the Synod.

II. *Election of delegates to the Synod.*—In the election of delegates to the Provincial Synod, the number of communicant members in the several churches on the New Year preceding said election shall be taken as the basis of representation at the Synod, and a certified copy of said number, signed by the ministers and the Church Committee

---

advisory committee of three, elected by the Synod, assists in the management. The income of the church is *barely* sufficient to cover the expenditures.

or Board of Elders, shall be sent in to the Provincial Elders' Conference prior to the holding of the Synod. Each church having less than one hundred and fifty communicant members, shall send one delegate; each church having one hundred and fifty communicants and less than three hundred, two delegates; each church having three hundred communicants and less than five hundred, three delegates; each church having five hundred communicants and less than seven hundred, shall be entitled to four delegates, and each church having seven hundred communicants or upward, shall be entitled to five delegates.

III. *Provincial Elders' Conference.*—The Provincial Elders' Conference shall consist of three members, who shall fill no special ministerial office in a single church, and shall be elected at each alternate Synod; and when that Synod shall have organized, the Provincial Elders' Conference shall resign their office.

IV. *Nomination of Bishops.*—In the nomination of Bishops, the choice of the Synod shall be expressed by ballot, and two-thirds of all the votes of members present shall be required for a nomination.

V. *Votes to fill vacancies in the Unity's Elders' Conference.*—The eight votes to which the Northern District of the American Province is entitled in filling vacancies which may occur in the Unity's Elders' Conference, shall be apportioned as follows:

The members of the Provincial Elders' Conference shall cast one vote; the ordained ministers in actual service at Bethlehem and Emmaus, one vote; the same at Nazareth, Schoeneck and Hopedale, one vote; the same at Litiz, Lancaster and Lebanon, one vote; the same at Philadelphia, York and Graceham, one vote; the same at New

York, Brooklyn and on Staten Island, one vote; the same in the churches of Ohio, one vote; the same in the churches of Indiana and Illinois, one vote; and if new churches be formed, the Provincial Elders' Conference shall have power to associate the ministers of the same with one or the other of the above classes, as they may think proper.

VI. *Finances.*—1. Every Provincial Synod shall elect a committee of three persons, who shall constitute an Advisory Board for the management of the secular affairs of the Sustentation Fund, in connection with the Provincial Elders' Conference.

2. In case of the resignation or death of any member of said committee, it shall have power to fill the vacancy until the next election.

3. It shall be the duty of said committee, in connection with the Provincial Elders' Conference, to hold monthly meetings; at which meetings a statement of the cash account shall be submitted by the Treasurer, and such part of the cash in hand as may be deemed advisable, be securely invested.

4. A statement of the financial affairs of the Sustentation Fund, and of the Church Boarding Schools, shall be presented to each Provincial Synod.

VII.—*Home Missions.*—The entire management of Home Missions, including the appointment of the Missionaries and the expenditure of all funds appropriated in aid of the Home Mission cause by the church, or contributed by societies or individuals, shall be entrusted to a "Home Mission Board;" which Board shall consist of the existing members of the Provincial Elders' Conference, and eight other persons, to be elected by each Synod, not less than three of whom shall be residents of the town of Bethlehem, in Pennsylvania. Said Board shall have power to fill vacancies in its own body.

VIII. *New Churches.*—New churches shall not be organized by division of existing churches, or colonization from the same, without the express sanction of the Provincial Synod.

B. CONSTITUTION OF THE SOUTHERN DISTRICT OF THE AMERICAN PROVINCE.

THE PROVINCIAL SYNOD.

The Provincial Synod shall meet statedly every six years, or more frequently, as the Synod or the Executive Board appointed by it may from time to time direct.

Powers of the Synod.

1. The Provincial Synod shall have power:

a. To examine the spiritual and temporal condition of the churches within the Province.

b. To adopt orders, rules and regulations for the government of the same.

c. To hear and redress grievances.

d. To examine and direct all financial matters of the Province, and prescribe rules for their management.

e. To prescribe the mode of nominating the bishops.

f. To elect delegates to the General Synod, according to the directions of the same.

g. Generally to direct all matters which belong to the government of the church within the Province.

2. Changes in the Constitution may be made by the Provincial Synod under the following restrictions:

Any proposed change in the Constitution shall be referred to a committee of nine brethren, elected by ballot, and when reported back from the committee, it shall be read and voted upon, on three separate days, and can only be passed by receiving at each reading a majority of three-fourths of the votes cast.

Organization of the Synod.

1. The churches of the Province shall be represented in the following ratio:

Every church shall be entitled to one delegate for every fifty communicant members; those churches, however, which have a less number of communicants, but still a separate organization, shall nevertheless be entitled to one delegate. *

2. Each Synod, when convened, shall be opened by the President of the existing Executive Board, but shall organize by electing its own president and other officers.

Members of the Synod.

The following shall be members of the Provincial Synod:

a. The members of the existing Executive Board.

b. The members of the Unity's Elders' Conference or the General Board of the whole Unity.

c. All bishops of the United Brethren's Church, whether in actual service or not.

* The rule in reference to organized churches is, *at this time*, as follows: A church with a separate organization, entitling it to a delegate in the Provincial Synod, is one that has a Standing Committee. No new church can be fully organized unless it numbers at least thirty communicants; whenever the number of communicant members of an existing church sinks below fifteen, then the separate organization of such a church is to be suspended in as far as its representation at the Synod is concerned.

d. All ordained brethren, who are in actual service in the Province, either as pastors of churches, or as principals of the educational institutions.

e. The financial agent of the Unity's Elders' Conference in the Province, commonly called the Administrator of the Unity.

f. The delegates from the different churches within the Province.

g. The members of the Provincial Boards of any other Province of the Brethren's Unity, or its delegates, and the delegates of other Provincial Synods of the Brethren's Church shall be entitled to seats, but as advisory members only, unless otherwise ordered.

h. Synod shall have the power to admit any other individual as an advisory, but not as a full member.

Provincial Elders' Conference.

1. At the stated Provincial Synod, to be convened every sixth year, this body shall elect, by ballot, two members of the Executive Board, which board is to be called the "Provincial Elders' Conference," and is to be responsible, in local matters, to the Provincial Synod.

2. The Provincial Elders' Conference shall consist of three members:

a. Of a president, who is to be chosen from the church at large, and who, as a general rule, is to hold no other office.

b. Of another member, to be elected from the ministers in the Province, whether in or out of office.

c. Of the administrator of the Unity's estates in N. C., who is appointed by the Unity's Elders' Conference.

3. It shall be the duty of the Provincial Elders' Conference:

a. To see to it that the general principles and regulations of the Brethren's Unity, as determined by the General Synods of the Church, as well as the rules, regulations and orders of the Provincial Synod are faithfully executed.

b. To supply the churches with the requisite pastors, under such rules and regulations as may be prescribed by the Provincial Synod.

c. To oversee the educational institutions.

d. To superintend the financial concerns of the Sustentation Fund, and the financial matters of the Province in general.

Vacancies in the Provincial Elders' Conference.

Vacancies which may occur in the Provincial Elders' Conference, during the interval between two stated Provincial Synods, shall be filled by a Provincial Synod to be convened for that purpose.

Finances of the Province.

The entire management of the Sustentation Fund of this Province shall be entrusted to a "Financial Board," composed of the Provincial Elders' Conference and three other members to be elected by the Provincial Synod at its stated meetings: vacancies occurring by death or otherwise among the three members thus elected, to be filled by the Board. Provided that nothing herein contained shall be construed as justifying the Financial Board in thwarting the action of the Provincial Elders' Conference, by refusing to defray the expenses necessarily incurred in such matters as belong to their duties as the Governing Board of the Province; as for instance, the formation and organization of new churches, the calling and appointing of ministers, &c.

From the Sustentation Fund shall be paid:

a. The salary of the President of the Provincial Elders' Conference, and the general expenses of this Conference and the Province.

b. The pensions of the superannuated ministers and others, who have been in the service of the church in the Province.

c. Any appropriations in aid of destitute churches.

d. The expenses of the general education of the children of ministers and others in the service of the church in the Province.

e. The expenses of the education of young men engaged in a course of theological study.*

C. CONSTITUTION OF THE CONTINENTAL PROVINCE.

THE PROVINCIAL SYNOD.

Powers of the Provincial Synod.

The Provincial Synod of the Continental Province shall have power:

a. To fix the time and place of meeting for the next Provincial Synod.

b. To direct and examine all financial matters of the Province.

c. To direct and control all the educational concerns of the Province.

d. To regulate the organization of new churches, and to change the constitution of existing churches.

e. To direct the home mission work in the Province, and the work of the Diaspora.

f. To direct and control all church publications in the Province, subject to the established doctrine and liturgy.

g. To hear and redress complaints and grievances.

* The Sustentation Fund consists almost exclusively of the sum received by this Province as its share on the final settlement and separation of the financial affairs of the Unity, at the General Synod of 1857. It is managed and controlled by the "Financial Board," which appoints a treasurer, who may or may not be a member of said Board.

Organization of the Provincial Synod.

The President of the existing Unity's Elders' Conference shall open the Synod; but the Synod shall organize by electing its own president and other officers.

Members of the Provincial Synod.

The following shall be members of the Continental Provincial Synod:

a. The members of the Unity's Elders' Conference.

b. The bishops of the Moravian Church residing in the Province.

c. The delegates of the churches, of which each church-settlement having a population of eight hundred souls, or more, shall send two, as also the settlement in the midst of which the Synod may be held; but every other church-settlement or church shall send one.

d. The deputies of the Elders' Conferences, each of which Conferences *must* be represented by one deputy.

e. The members of the Elders' Conference in the settlement in which the Synod is held, of whom, however, only one shall have a vote, as the representative of that Conference.

f. Delegates of other Provinces of the Unity, and such other brethren as the Unity's Elders' Conference, in its capacity of Provincial Conference may invite, shall be advisory members, but have no vote.

THE PROVINCIAL ELDERS' CONFERENCE.

Until the meeting of the next General Synod, the Unity's Elders' Conference shall, at the same time, be the Provincial Elders' Conference of the Continental Province, and as such, responsible to the Synod of that Province; exercising in the Continental Province the same powers which the other Provincial Elders' Conferences hold in their respective Provinces.

D. CONSTITUTION OF THE BRITISH PROVINCE.

THE PROVINCIAL SYNOD.

1. The Provincial Synod of the British Province shall have power:

a. To fix the time and place of meeting for the next Provincial Synod.

b. To direct and examine all financial matters of the Province.

c. To direct and control all the educational concerns of the Province.

d. To regulate the organization of new churches, and to change the constitution of existing churches.

e. To direct the home mission work in the Province.

f. To direct and control all church publications in the Province, subject to the established doctrine and liturgy.

g. To hear and redress complaints and grievances.

h. To elect the Provincial Elders' Conference, which shall consist of three brethren; and two-thirds of the votes shall be necessary to a choice.

2. At the Provincial Synod of the British Province, the President of the Provincial Elders' Conference shall preside.

3. The following shall be members of this Provincial Synod:

a. The members of the Provincial Elders' Conference.

b. The bishops in the Province.

c. The Advocatus and Secretarius Fratrum.

d. The agent of the Foreign Missions.

e. Members of Elders' Conferences, and ministers who can leave their place of residence without prejudice to the office they hold.

f. Delegates from the churches, each church having the right to choose one.

g. Members of the Unity's Elders' Conference, and the delegates of other Provinces shall be advisory members, but without a vote.

THE PROVINCIAL ELDERS' CONFERENCE.

1. The Provincial Elders' Conference of this Province shall resign at each Provincial Synod, which shall elect a new board, the former members being re-eligible. One of the elected members shall be appointed President by the Unity's Elders' Conference.

2. This Provincial Elders' Conference shall be subordinate and responsible to the Unity's Elders' Conference.

3. In case of a vacancy occurring in the Provincial Elders' Conference, it shall be filled by the Unity's Elders' Conference, guided by the votes of the ministers of the Province, together with a vote of each church-committee.

CHANGE OF CONSTITUTION.

No proposition affecting the constitution of the British Provincial Synod, or the Provincial Elders' Conference, shall be brought forward in a Provincial Synod, unless it has, three months previously, been communicated by its author to the Provincial Elders' Conference, and through them to the churches of the British Province.

SECTION III.—THE USE OF THE LOT.

As this subject refers particularly to the ecclesiastical government of the church, a brief account of the principles upon which the use of the Lot is based, must be appended to the chapter on Constitution.

The use of the lot, in the Moravian Church, is neither a mysterious, theosophic appliance, nor an exclusive right and prerogative bestowed upon that particular communion; but simply a Scriptural act of faith, which any body of Christians may perform. We find, indeed, no express command given in the New Testament, nor even a direct promise, in regard to it. But Christ declares: "Therefore I say unto you, What things soever ye desire when ye pray, believe that ye receive them, and ye shall have them." (Mark xi. 24.) And in the Acts of the Apostles, the following record occurs: "And they appointed two, Joseph called Barsabas, who was surnamed Justus, and Matthias. And they prayed, and said, Thou, Lord, which knowest the hearts of all men, show whether of these two thou hast chosen, that he may take part of this ministry and apostleship, from which Judas by transgression fell, that he might go to his own place. And they gave forth their lots; and the lot fell upon Matthias; and he was numbered with the eleven apostles." (Acts i. 23–26.) Upon this promise of Christ, and practice of the apostles, the use of the lot, in the Moravian Church, is founded. The church believes that God *permits* it, as long as it is upheld by faith. As soon as a majority of Moravian ministers and people declare that they no longer have confidence in this mode of determining the will of the Lord, it must necessarily be abolished. This essential condition of the use of the lot has been repeatedly recognized by the General Synod. Here follows the substance of the declaration of the last General Synod, held in 1857, in reference to this matter:

"The means by which our Lord and Saviour conducts his government in the Brethren's Church are no other than those by which he rules his universal church; namely, his Holy Word, his Holy Spirit, who leads us into all truth, and the dispensations of his Providence, by which he determines the course of his church, and of each individual, according to his own wisdom and love. But if we are to be led by them, there is required on our part a heart obedient to the direction of his Word, an ear open to receive the instruction of his Spirit, and a watchful eye to mark the intimations which He gives us in the leadings of his Providence. The more these dispositions are wrought in our hearts through grace, the more securely shall we be able to follow his guidance. Such was the conviction of our forefathers, from the first establishment of our union. Nevertheless, there were peculiar cases in which, deeply convinced of the insufficiency of their own insight into the things of God, and his government of his church, and animated by an earnest desire to know the will of the Lord, and to be guided by him alone, they had recourse to the lot, believing that our Saviour would not put their child-like confidence to shame, (Mark xi. 24,) but in answer to their united prayers, would by this means reveal to them his gracious will. This use of the lot is not founded on any express command or promise in the Scriptures of the New Testament. We read, however, in the Acts of the Apostles, that the lot was used by them in the appointment of Matthias to the apostolic office. This example of the apostles determined the founders of the Ancient Moravian Church to refer to the lot the choice of their first three elders, and the congregation of Herrnhut followed the same precedent, when, on May 20th, 1727, they chose by lot, four brethren out of twelve proposed for the office of elder. Afterwards the use of the lot was continued in the choice of elders, and the sending out of missionaries and other messengers of the church. And not only in these cases, but in all affairs of importance, as the congregation of Herrnhut gradually expanded into the Unity of the Brethren, those who had the direction of it, felt the necessity of being thus guided."

"We regard the lot with thankfulness, as a means granted to us for the time, by the Lord, for learning his mind, and acting under his direction, when He does not give us to know His will in any other way. Should filial confidence in this special guidance of our Lord become more and more weakened among us, it would be time to lay aside a usage, which must be devoid of blessing, as soon as it ceases to be grounded on the innermost conviction of the heart." (Synodal Results of 1857, § 41.)

The use of the lot, as it affects the whole Unity, takes place in the two following cases:

1. The election or appointment of bishops, as a general rule, is submitted to the lot.

2. The election of a new member of the Unity's Elders' Conference, to fill a vacancy in that body, occurring in the interval between two General Synods, is always submitted to the lot.

Each Province has particular rules governing the use of the lot. Those for the American Province are the following:

1. When the members of the Provincial Elders' Conference, after deliberating on an appointment, are *fully* and *unanimously* convinced, that they desire, in sincere faith, for *themselves*, the direction of the Lord through the lot, then they may ask the question by the lot, but such use of the lot shall be binding on the Provincial Elders' Conference only, and not on the person to whom the appointment is offered.

2. When a brother or sister receives an appointment from the Provincial Elders' Conference, and requires a

special lot for his or her direction, he or she may ask the Provincial Elders' Conference, in writing, to have a special lot cast for himself or herself, and the directions given by the lot shall be absolutely binding upon that brother or sister.

3. When a brother or sister is desirous of having in his or her *private affairs* a decision by lot, the use of the lot shall be allowed, provided the Provincial Elders' Conference becomes satisfied that the applicant for its use is possessed of implicit faith and confidence, and will yield perfect obedience to and cheerful acquiescence in the Lord's will thus ascertained; and provided further, that the matter concerning which the lot is requested, be of such a nature as to render its use proper in the estimation of the Provincial Elders' Conference.—*Synodal Results of* 1857, § 44.

These simple and explicit regulations set forth the limits* within which the use of the lot is allowed in this

* The use of the lot in contracting marriages was abolished, as a rule, many years ago. Much has been said and written on this subject by persons not acquainted with the true state of the case, and attempts have been made to cast ridicule upon the usage. This note is given in the way of explanation of the usage, as it really prevailed.

The fundamental principle underlying the employment of the lot in the case of marriages, was a noble principle of devotion to the service of Christ. The Brethren believed that the extension of His kingdom, through their agency, should not be hindered by any of the relations of this life, in accordance with what the Lord himself said, as stated in Matthew, xix. 29. They feared that early engagements would often prevent young men from going forth, as messengers of the gospel, to distant lands, or render a long abode in them irksome; they were, moreover, convinced

Province, and imply that it is never to be employed by an individual, or by any other ecclesiastical board or body, except the Provincial Elders' Conference, and the Provincial Synod.

that it was a matter of the utmost importance not only to enter the marriage state in the fear of God, but to secure partners in life who would, in the fullest sense, be helpmates to them while laboring in the Lord's vineyard. Therefore they had faith in Him that he would condescend to give them such wives as they needed, and as would approve themselves worthy handmaids of His. Besides, owing to the peculiar regulations of the settlements, young men and young women had very little social intercourse together. In this way, the lot came into use for contracting marriages in the case of missionaries and ministers, and gradually of all the members of the church. But it was not employed in the manner so often set forth by ignorant writers. Men and women were not indiscriminately coupled, without their knowledge, and contrary to their wishes. The mode of proceeding was simply this: When a man wished to marry, *he proposed* a woman to the authorities of the church; or, if he had no proposal to make, left it to them to suggest a woman. The authorities submitted the proposal to the decision of the lot, and if it was confirmed, made the woman an offer of marriage in the name of the man, which offer she was at perfect liberty to reject, if she thought proper; for the lot bound the authorities to make the offer, but not the woman to accept it. If she refused, or if the proposal was negatived by the lot, the man made another; and the authorities never forced any woman upon him against his will.

So far, therefore, from ridiculing this usage, an intelligent mind capable of appreciating the spirit which animated the early Brethren in this respect, will be filled with profound admiration at the faith which they displayed. When confidence in this mode of contracting marriages began to wane, the rule was abrogated. But while it continued, there were far less *unhappy* marriages among the Brethren, than among the same number of people in any other denomination of Christians. This is a well known and abundantly substantiated fact.

In fifth line from heading, Chapter IV, read 1536 in place of 1564.

CHAPTER IV.

DOCTRINE.

INTRODUCTION.

The Ancient Church of the Brethren had a regular Confession of Faith, which was several times revised, and appeared in its most complete form in the year 1535. In 1564, it was published in German, with a preface by Dr. M. Luther. The Renewed Church has no Confession of Faith, as such; that is, no document bearing this name. In the Continental Province, where adherence to a Confession is an essential condition of the ecclesiastical privileges which the Brethren's Church enjoys, the Augsburg Confession, in its twenty-one articles, is acknowledged, "being the first and most generally received Confession of the Protestant Church, and containing a simple and clear enunciation of the articles of the Christian faith."* This acknowledgment, however, according to the declaration of the General Synod, does not bind the conscience of any member, much less is it of any account in those Provinces of the Unity "where the Augsburg Confession has no other value than as being the creed of one (the Lutheran)

* Synodal Results of 1857, § 94, p. 96.

among many churches enjoying equal rights and liberty."*

But although the Moravian Brethren's Church has issued no Confession of Faith, as such, it has several works, bearing the authority of the General Synod, and setting forth the doctrines which it teaches. These are: "An Exposition of Christian Doctrine as taught in the Protestant Church of the United Brethren," by Bishop Spangenberg, Barby, 1779, translated into English by La Trobe, and published in 1784; "A Catechism for the Instruction of Youth in the Church of the United Brethren," various editions, German and English; "An Epitome of Christian Doctrine for the Instruction of Candidates for Confirmation;" and a chapter on Doctrine, in the Synodal Results. "The Easter Morning Litany," moreover, contains a brief Confession of Faith, and is used annually in all Moravian churches in Christian and heathen lands.

A Compendium of Doctrine is here given, compiled from the authorized publications of the church, and in their very languages, with references to the works from which the sentences are severally taken. Then follows the Easter Morning Litany.

A COMPENDIUM OF DOCTRINE.

I.—*Of the Standard of Doctrine.*

The Holy Scriptures, of the Old and New Testament, are and remain the only rule of our faith and practice. We

* Synodal Results of 1857, § 94, p. 96.

revere them as the word of God, which he spake to mankind, in time past by the prophets, and in these last days by his Son and his apostles, to instruct them in the way of salvation through faith in Christ Jesus.*

II.—*Of the Holy Trinity.*

We believe that God revealed himself to man, as Father, Son, and Holy Ghost. (Matt. xxviii. 19.)†

III.—*Of God the Father.*

The most exalted character we can give of the Father, is that he is the Father of our Lord Jesus Christ; (2 Cor. xi. 31; Ephes i. 3; 1 Peter i. 3;)‡ hence we hold the doctrine of the love of God the Father, who "has chosen us in Christ before the foundation of the world," and who "so loved the world that he gave his only begotten Son, that whosoever believeth in him should not perish, but have everlasting life."§

IV.—*Of God the Son.*

We hold the doctrine of the real Godhead and real manhood of Jesus Christ; that God the Creator of all things, was manifested in the flesh, and has reconciled the world unto himself; that "he is before all things, and by him all things consist."||

V.—*Of God the Holy Ghost.*

We hold the doctrine of the Holy Ghost and his gracious

* Synodal Results of 1857, § 4, p. 6.
† Catechism for Confirmation, Question 4.
‡ Spangenberg's Exposition, § 86, p. 140.
§ Synodal Results of 1857, § 6, p. 7.
|| Synodal Results of 1857, § 6, p. 7.

operations,* who proceedeth from the Father, and whom our Lord Jesus Christ sent after he went away, that he should abide with us forever;† and believe that it is he who works in us the knowledge of sin, faith in Jesus, and the witness that we are children of God.‡

VI.—*Of Total Depravity.*

We hold the doctrine of the total depravity of human nature; that there is no health in us; and that, since the fall, we have no power left to save ourselves.§

VII.—*Of the Atonement.*

We hold the doctrine of the atonement and satisfaction of Jesus Christ for us; that he "was delivered for our offences, and was raised again for our justification;" and that in his merits alone we find forgiveness of sins and peace with God.||

VIII.—*Of the New Birth.*

It has been the earnest desire of our church, from the beginning, that each individual member of it should be led, in the school of the Holy Ghost, to a deep and thorough knowledge, not only of his sinfulness, but of his exposedness to condemnation before God, as the desert of sin; and so be brought to genuine repentance, and to the conviction of his need of a Saviour; whence will result, through living faith in Jesus, a thorough renewal of the inward man, consisting not in the mere laying aside of

* Synodal Results of 1857, § 6, p. 8.
† Easter Morning Litany, p. xv.
‡ Synodal Results of 1857, § 6, p. 8.
§ Synodal Results of 1857, § 6, p. 7.
|| Synodal Results of 1856, § 6, p. 7.

some sinful habits, but in an entire change of views and dispositions, and in a full surrender of the heart to the Lord.*

IX.—*Of Faith*

Cordially to embrace that faithful saying, as worthy of all acceptation, that Christ Jesus came into the world to save sinners, and that for the sake of his blood and death, *our* sins are forgiven, and life and salvation imparted unto *us*—this is faith, the gift of God, coming not by our own reason and strength. We believe, that through faith we obtain righteousness and peace with God, for Christ's sake, and the sure hope of eternal life and happiness.†

X.—*Of Sanctification.*

We hold the doctrine of the fruits of faith, that it must show itself as an active principle, by a willing obedience to God's commandments, flowing from love and gratitude to God;‡ and believe that it is necessary for the pardoned sinner to maintain close and constant communion with our Saviour, according to his own words: "As the branch cannot bear fruit of itself, except it abide in the vine, no more can ye, except ye abide in me," (John xv. 4); that thus true sanctification of soul and body, and a transformation into the Saviour's image, are wrought within us, not legally, but evangelically; and that the work is cherished in humility, and maintained and ripened more and more for the perfect state, by a constant looking unto Jesus, and to all the merits of his holy life.§

* Synodal Results of 1857, § 8, p. 8 and 9.

† Catechism for Confirmation, Questions 26, 27 and 28.

‡ Synodal Results of 1857, § 6, p. 8.

§ Synodal Results of 1857, § 8. p. 9.

XI.—*Of Jesus Christ as the Centre of Doctrine.*

In conformity with these fundamental articles of our faith, the great theme of our preaching is Jesus Christ our Saviour, he who says of the Scriptures: "they are they which testify of me,"—"in whom all the promises of God are yea and amen,"—in whom we have the grace of the Son, the love of the Father, and the communion of the Holy Ghost. The word of the cross—that is, the testimony of his voluntary offering of himself to suffer and to die, and of the treasures of grace purchased thereby—is the beginning, middle and end of our ministry, and to proclaim the Lord's death we regard as the main calling of the Brethren's Church. We point to him as "made of God unto us wisdom, and righteousness, and sanctification, and redemption." Hence we maintain, that while the law of God is given us for the knowledge of sin, we are led to true contrition of spirit by the testimony which the Holy Ghost bears more especially to our want of faith in Jesus, and our indifference to the Saviour who hung upon the cross for us. (John xvi. 8 and 9; Acts ix. 5.) The look at his agonizing death shows us the merited curse and condemnation under which we lie by nature, but at the same time reveals the sole ground of justification before God, reconciliation with him, and deliverance from the power of death, and from our vain conversation, so that the conscience is "purged from dead works to serve the living God."*

XII.—*Of Christian Life.*

Our great and only Master comprises the whole doctrine of Christian morality, according to its inmost spirit,

* Synodal Results of 1857, § 7, p. 8.

in the commandment of love to God, and to our neighbor. After his example and that of his apostles, we will be careful to remind one another of all those Christian virtues which flow therefrom, and which adorn the character of a true child of God. We will especially enforce the importance of strict conscientiousness in our whole conduct, and raise a warning voice against every species of vice and immorality. Yet all our warnings and exhortations must not only have reference to Jesus as our all-perfect example, but be in close accordance with the doctrine of faith, insisting, according to our Lord's direction, that the tree must first be made good, in order that it may bring forth good fruit.*

XIII.—*Of the Church.*

The souls dispersed in all the world, who adhere to Christ by faith, who are partakers of the Holy Ghost, and worship the Father in spirit and in truth, are the body of Christ, the house of God, the flock of the Good Shepherd,†—the holy, universal Christian Church.‡

XIV.—*Of Baptism.*

We first receive a pledge of the forgiveness of sins, and of the grace of God in Christ Jesus, in the sacrament of Holy Baptism, for baptism is a washing and cleansing from sin by the blood of Jesus Christ, who loved the church, and gave himself for it, that he might sanctify and cleanse it with the washing of water by the word.§ (Ephes. v. 25 and 26.)

* Synodal Results of 1857, § 9, p. 10.

† Spangenberg's Exposition, § 254, p. 441.

‡ Easter Morning Litany, p. xv.

§ Catechism for Confirmation, Question 33 and 34.

XV.—*Of the Baptism of Infants.*

Infant Baptism is, in the Holy Scriptures, neither expressly commanded nor forbidden;* but inasmuch as our children, by their birth in the Christian church, are called by the Lord to participate in the blessings of the Gospel Dispensation, (1 Cor. vii. 14,) and Christ himself blessed little children, and declared that of such was the kingdom of heaven, we consider it to be the duty of parents to bring their infants to be baptized.†

XVI.—*Of the Lord's Supper.*

The promise of the forgiveness of sins and the grace of God is renewed and sealed to us, in the sacrament of the Lord's Supper;—which is a memorial of his death, instituted by Christ himself, wherein, while jointly eating of the blessed bread and drinking of the blessed cup, we receive the body and blood of our Lord Jesus Christ, as a pledge of the forgiveness of sins, of life, and eternal happiness.‡ (1 Cor. xi. 26, x. 16.) That is, whenever this Holy Supper is taken according to the mind of Jesus Christ, the enjoyment of the bread and wine is connected with the enjoyment of the body and blood of Jesus, in a manner incomprehensible to us, and therefore inexpressible.§

XVII.—*Of the Final Condition of Mankind in Eternity.*

The wicked, condemned by Christ, the righteous Judge, shall suffer everlasting punishment in hell; but the righteous shall see God, and be forever with the Lord, in whose

* Spangenberg's Exposition, § 141 p. 235.

† Synodal Results of 1857, § 19.

‡ Catechism for Confirmation, Question 37 and 38.

§ Spangenberg's Exposition, § 146, p. 245.

presence there is fulness of joy, and at whose right hand there are pleasures for evermore. (Matt. xxv. 34, 41, 46; 1 Thess. iv. 17.*

THE EASTER MORNING LITANY.

MIN. I believe in the One only God, Father, Son, and Holy Ghost, who created all things by Jesus Christ, and was in Christ, reconciling the world unto himself.

I believe in God, the Father of our Lord Jesus Christ, who hath chosen us in him before the foundation of the world;

Who hath delivered us from the power of darkness, and hath translated us into the kingdom of his dear Son;

Who hath blessed us with all spiritual blessings in heavenly places in Christ;

Who hath made us meet to be partakers of the inheritance of the saints in light: having predestinated us unto the adoption of children by Jesus Christ to himself, according to the good pleasure of his will, to the praise of the glory of his grace, wherein he hath made us accepted in the Beloved.

CONG. *This I verily believe.*

We thank thee, O Father, Lord of heaven and earth, because thou hast hid these things from the wise and prudent, and hast revealed them unto babes: even so, Father; for so it seemed good in thy sight.

Father, glorify thy name.

MIN. AND CONG. *Our Father which art in heaven, hallowed be thy name; thy kingdom come; thy will be done in earth, as it is in heaven: give us this day our daily bread; and forgive us our trespasses, as we forgive them*

* Catechism for Confirmation, Question 41.

that trespass against us; and lead us not into temptation, but deliver us from evil: for thine is the kingdom, and the power, and the glory, for ever and ever: Amen.

MIN. I believe in the name of the only begotten Son of God, by whom are all things, and we through him;

I believe, that he was made flesh, and dwelled among us, and took on him the form of a servant;

By the overshadowing of the Holy Ghost, was conceived of the Virgin Mary; as the children are partakers of flesh and blood, he also himself likewise took part of the same; was born of a woman;

And being found in fashion as a man, was tempted in all points like as we are, yet without sin:

For he is the Lord, the Messenger of the covenant, whom we delight in. The Lord and his Spirit hath sent him to proclaim the acceptable year of the Lord:

He spoke that which he did know, and testified that which he had seen: as many as received him, to them gave he the power to become the sons of God.

Behold the Lamb of God, which taketh away the sins of the world;

Suffered under Pontius Pilate, was crucified, dead, and buried;

The third day rose again from the dead, and with him many bodies of the saints which slept;

Ascended into heaven, and sitteth on the throne of the Father, whence he will come, in like manner as he was seen going into heaven.

CONG. Amen, come, Lord Jesus; come, we implore thee:
With longing hearts we now are waiting for thee;
Come soon, O come.

The Lord will descend from heaven with a shout, with

the voice of the archangel, and with the trump of God, to judge both the quick and the dead.

This is my Lord, who redeemed me, a lost and undone human creature, purchased and gained me from sin, from death, and from the power of the devil;

Not with gold or silver, but with his holy precious blood, and with his innocent suffering and dying;

To the end that I should be his own, and in his kingdom live under him and serve him, in eternal righteousness, innocence, and happiness;

So as he, being risen from the dead, liveth and reigneth, world without end.

CONG. *This I most certainly believe.*

I believe in the Holy Ghost, who proceedeth from the Father, and whom our Lord Jesus Christ sent, after he went away, that he should abide with us for ever;

That he should comfort us, as a mother comforteth her children;

That he should help our infirmities, and make intercession for us with groanings which cannot be uttered;

That he should bear witness with our spirit, that we are the children of God, and teach us to cry, Abba, Father:

That he should shed abroad in our hearts the love of God, and make our bodies his holy temple:

And that he should work all in all, dividing to every man severally as he will.

To him be glory in the church, which is in Christ Jesus, the holy, universal Christian church, in the communion of saints, at all times, and from eternity to eternity.

CONG. *Amen.*

I believe that, by my own reason and strength, I cannot believe in Jesus Christ my Lord, or come to him;

But that the Holy Ghost calleth me by the gospel, enlighteneth me with his gifts, sanctifieth and preserveth me in the true faith;

Even as he calleth, gathereth, enlighteneth, and sanctifieth the whole church on earth, which he keepeth by Jesus Christ in the only true faith;

In which Christian church, God forgiveth me and every believer all sin daily and abundantly.

CONG. *This I assuredly believe.*

I believe, that by holy baptism I am embodied as a member of the church of Christ, which he hath loved, and for which he gave himself, that he might sanctify and cleanse it with the washing of water by the word.

CONG. *Amen.*

In this communion of saints my faith is placed upon my Lord and Saviour Jesus Christ, who died for us, and shed his blood on the cross for the remission of sins, and who hath granted unto me his body and blood in the Lord's Supper, as a pledge of grace; as the Scriptures saith, our Lord Jesus Christ, the same night in which he was betrayed, took bread: and when he had given thanks, he brake it, and gave it to his disciples, and said, Take, eat: this is my body which is given for you; this do in remembrance of me. After the same manner also, our Lord Jesus Christ, when he had supped, took the cup, gave thanks, and gave it to them, saying, Drink ye all of it: this is my blood, the blood of the New Testament, which is shed for you, and for many, for the remission of sins. This do ye, as oft as ye drink it, in remembrance of me.

CONG. *Amen.*

I have a desire to depart, and to be with Christ, which

is far better; I shall never taste death; yea, I shall attain unto the resurrection of the dead: for the body which I shall put off, this grain of corruptibility, shall put on incorruption; my flesh shall rest in hope.

And the God of peace, that brought again from the dead our Lord Jesus, that great Shepherd of the sheep, through the blood of the everlasting covenant, shall also quicken these our mortal bodies, if so be that the Spirit of God hath dwelled in them.

CONG. *Amen.*

We poor sinners pray,
Hear us, gracious Lord and God;

And keep us in everlasting fellowship with our brethren, and with our sisters, who have entered into the joy of their Lord;

Also with the servants and handmaids of our church, whom thou hast called home in the past year, and with the whole church triumphant; and let us rest together in thy presence from our labors.

CONG. *Amen.*

They are at rest in lasting bliss,
Beholding Christ our Saviour:
Our humble expectation is
To live with him for ever.

Glory be to Him who is the Resurrection and the Life; He was dead, and behold, He is alive for evermore; And he that believeth in Him, though he were dead, yet shall he live.

Glory be to Him in the church which waiteth for Him, and in that which is around Him; for ever and ever.

CONG. *Amen.*

Grant us to lean unshaken
  Upon thy faithfulness,
Until we hence are taken
  To see thee face to face.

The grace of our Lord Jesus Christ, and the love of God, and the communion of the Holy Ghost, be with us all.

CONG. *Amen.*

CHAPTER V.

MINISTRY.

THE orders in the ministry of the Moravian United Brethren's Church, are derived from the Ancient Unitas Fratrum, and are those of *Bishops*, *Presbyters* and *Deacons*.

I. *Bishops.*—The episcopal succession, which was secured in the manner set forth in the first chapter, is prized by the church as a valuable inheritance, and as one of the principal links which connect the former and the present Unity. But the prerogatives of the episcopal office, as it now exists, are different from those formerly connected with it. In the Ancient Church, the government was vested, ex officio, in the bishops. This is not the case now. The Renewed Church had adopted a form of government before the episcopate was transferred to it; and when the transfer took place, no change was made in that form. The General Synod has established the following principles:

1. "Our episcopacy in itself gives to the individual who holds it, no title to a share in the government of the Brethren's Church, or of any individual congregation.

2. "No bishop is, as such, subordinate to another.

3. "A bishop has no diocese committed to his jurisdiction.

4. "A bishop, like every other servant of the Unity, must receive a special appointment to any office which he holds, from the Synod, or the Unity's Elders' Conference, or a Provincial Elders' Conference.

5. "Ordination to the different church-degrees can be performed only by virtue of an express commission from the above-mentioned authorities."

The prerogatives belonging to the bishops, in virtue of their office, are:

1. They only can ordain to the three orders in the ministry.

2. They have a seat and vote in the General Synod.

3. They have a seat and vote in the Provincial Synods of the respective Provinces in which they reside.

At the same time, however, bishops are almost invariably, by election or appointment, connected with the government of the church, both in the Provinces and so far as the Unity at large is concerned. The President of the Unity's Elders' Conference, with only two exceptions, has always been a bishop; and the Presidents of the Provincial Elders' Conferences, as a general thing, belong to the same order. There are at present sixteen bishops, of whom three have retired from active service. Of the thirteen in the service, eight are engaged in administering the government of the church; namely, four in the Unity's Elders' Conference, two in the Provincial Conference of the American Province North, and two in the Provincial Conference of the British Province.

Bishops are elected by the General Synod, or appointed by the Unity's Elders' Conference. In either case, the lot, as a general rule, is used. The American Province has the right to nominate its bishops, which is done by the Provincial Synod; but the appointment rests with the General Synod, or Unity's Elders' Conference.

II. *Presbyters.*—When deacons, after serving one or two years, have approved themselves worthy ministers of Christ and his church, and have charge of a congregation, or are appointed to preside over any distinct branch of service in the Brethren's Church, they are ordained presbyters. This ordination does not give them any new prerogatives, but confirms them in their ministerial office.

III. *Deacons.*—The degree of deacon is conferred upon candidates for the ministry, when they first enter the service of the church; and this ordination qualifies them for administering the sacraments.

The "Synodal Results" of 1857 contain the following sentiment respecting ordination to these three orders: "As every ordination is accompanied by the believing prayers of the assembled congregation, to the Head of the church, and by the laying on of hands in the name of the Father, the Son, and the Holy Ghost, we consider it as a means of conveying special divine blessing to those who receive the important charge, to feed the church of God, which He has purchased with his own blood."

Candidates for the Ministry.—In the American Province, such young men as have finished their studies in the Theological Seminary, and passed the examinations which are held, semi-annually, in this institution, become candidates for the ministry, and are thereby licensed to preach. They generally enter the Church Boarding School at Nazareth, as teachers, and remain there until they receive appointments as ministers.

In the other Provinces of the Unity, candidates for the ministry are usually received into *the class of acolothists*, which has been derived from the Ancient Brethren's Church. Into the same class many of the instructors of youth, female elders, and superintendents of Widows' and Sisters' Houses, wives of missionaries and of ministers are admitted. The reception takes place in the presence of the Unity's Elders' Conference, or of a Provincial Elders' Conference; the persons received giving their right hands to the elders, as a pledge of their desire to be faithful in the service of the church. This custom is occasionally observed in the American Province.

Here follows the episcopal succession, from the beginning of the Ancient Unitas Fratrum to the present time. Stephen, Bishop of the Waldenses, and his assistants, transferred the succession to the Ancient Church, in the year 1467, consecrating the first three bishops of the list below; and Daniel Jablonsky and Christian Sitkovius, the survivors of the line, transferred the succession to the Renewed Church, in the year 1735, consecrating David Nitschman, the first bishop of the present Unity. It will be seen from this list, that the Moravian Church is the oldest Protestant Episcopal church. In the year 1749, the Parliament of Great Britain passed an act to encourage the Brethren to settle in North America, and acknowledged them as an episcopal church.

The Episcopal Succession of the Unitas Fratrum, from 1467 *to* 1859.

No.	Year of Consecration.	Bishops.	Provinces.
		Ancient Church.	
1	1467	Michael Bradacius,	Moravian-Bohemian.
2	"	A Waldensian Pastor,	" "
3	"	A Roman Catholic Priest,	" "
4	"	Matthias of Kunwalde,	" "
5	"	Procop of Hradeck,	" "
6	1499	Thomas of Przelautsch,	" "
7	"	Elias of Krzizanow,	" "
8	1503	Luke of Prague,	" "
9	"	Ambrose of Skutsch,	" "
10	1506	Wenzel,	" "
11	"	Daniel,	" "
12	1516	Martin Skoda,	" "
13	1529	Wenzel Albus,	" "
14	"	Andrew Cyclov,	" "
15	"	John Horn,	" "
16	1532	Benedict Bavorin,	" "

No.	Year of Consecration.	Bishops.	Provinces.
17	1532	Veit Michalek,	Moravian-Bohemian.
18	"	John Augusta,	" "
19	1537	Martin Michalek,	" "
20	"	Matthias Sion,	" "
21	1550	John Czerny,	" "
22	"	Matthias,	" "
23	"	Paul Paulin,	" "
24	1553	Matthias Czervenka,	" "
25	1557	George Israel,	Polish.
26	"	John Blahoslav,	Moravian-Bohemian.
27	1571	Andrew Stephan,	" "
28	"	Jan Caleph,	" "
29	"	Jan Lorenz,	Polish.
30	1577	Zacharias of Leitomischl,	Moravian-Bohemian.
31	"	John Aeneas,	" "
32	1587	John Abdias,	" "
33	"	Simon Theophilus Turnovsky,	Polish.
34	1589	John Ephraim,	Moravian-Bohemian.
35	"	Paul Jessen,	" "
36	1594	Jacob Narciss,	" "
37	"	Jan Niemczansky,	" "
38	1599	Samuel Sussitzky,	" "
39	"	Zacharias Ariston,	" "
40	1601	Bartholomew Niemczansky,	" "
41	"	Jan Lanetsch,	" "
42	1606	Jan Cruciger,	" "
43	1608	Martin Gratian Gertich,	Polish.
44	"	Matthias Rybinsky,	"
45	1609	Matthias Koneczny,	Moravian-Bohemian.
46	1611	Matthias Cyrus,	" "
47	1612	John Turnovsky,	Polish.
48	"	Gregory Erastus,	Moravian-Bohemian.
49	1618	John Cyrill,	" "
50	1627	Daniel Micolajivsky,	Polish.
51	1629	Paul Paliurus,	"
52	1632	Lawrence Justin,	Moravian-Bohemian.
53	"	Matthias Procop,	" "
54	"	John Amos Comenius,	" "
55	"	Paul Fabricius,	Polish.
56	1633	Martin Orminsky,	"
57	"	John Rybinsky,	"
58	1644	Martin Gertich, jun.	"

No.	Year of Consecration.	Bishops.	Provinces.
59	1644	John Buettner,	Polish.
60	1662	Nicholas Gertich,	"
61	"	Peter Jablonsky,	"
62	1673	Adam Samuel Hartman,	"
63	1676	John Zugehoer,	"
64	1692	Joachim Gulich,	"
65	1699	John Jacobides,	"
66	"	Daniel Ernst Jablonsky,	"
67	1709	Solomon Opitz,	"
68	1712	David Cassius,	"
69	1725	Paul Cassius,	"
70	1734	Christian Sitkov,	"
		RENEWED CHURCH.	
71	1735	David Nitschman,	American.
72	1737	Lewis Count de Zinzendorf,	Continental.
73	1740	Polycarp Mueller,	"
74	1741	John Nitschman, sen.	American.
75	1743	Frederick Baron de Wattewille,	Continental.
76	1744	Martin Dober,	"
77	1745	Augustus G. Spangenberg,	American.
78	1746	David Nitschman, jun.	Continental.
79	"	Frederick W. Neisser,	"
80	"	Christian F. Steinhofer,	"
81	"	J. F. Camerhof,	American.
82	1747	John Baron de Wattewille,	Continental.
83	"	Leonard Dober,	"
84	"	A. A. Vieroth,	"
85	1748	Frederick Martin,	West Indies.
86	"	Peter Boehler,	American.
87	1750	George Waiblinger,	Continental.
88	1751	Matthew Hehl,	American.
89	1754	John Gambold,	British.
90	1756	Andrew Grasman,	Continental.
91	1758	John Nitschman,	"
92	"	Nathaniel Seidel,	American.
93	1770	Martin Mack,	West Indies.
94	1773	Martin Graf,	American.
95	1775	John F. Reichel,	Continental.
96	"	Paul E. Layritz,	"
97	"	P. H. Molther,	"
98	1782	Henry de Brueningk,	"

No.	Year of Consecration.	Bishops.	Provinces.
99	1782	George Clemens,	Continental.
100	"	Jeremiah Risler,	"
101	1783	George Tranecker,	British.
102	1784	John Etwein,	American.
103	1785	John Schaukirch,	West Indies.
104	1786	Benjamin G. Mueller,	Continental.
105	1789	Christian Gregor,	"
106	"	Samuel Liebisch,	"
107	"	C. Duvernoy,	"
108	"	Benjamin Rothe,	"
109	1790	John A. Huebner,	American.
110	"	John D. Koehler,	"
111	1801	Thomas Moore,	British.
112	"	Christian Dober,	Continental.
113	"	Samuel T. Benade,	British.
114	"	Gotthold Reichel,	American.
115	1802	George H. Loskiel,	"
116	1808	John G. Cunow,	Continental.
117	"	Herman Richter,	"
118	1811	John Herbst,	American.
119	1814	William Fabricius,	Continental.
120	"	Charles G. Hueffel,	American.
121	"	Charles A. Baumeister,	Continental.
122	"	John Baptiste de Albertini,	"
123	1815	Jacob Van Vleck,	American.
124	1818	George M. Schneider,	Continental.
125	"	F. W. Foster,	British.
126	"	Benjamin Reichel,	Continental.
127	1822	Andrew Benade,	American.
128	1825	John Wied,	Continental.
129	"	Lewis Fabricius,	"
130	"	Peter F. Curie,	"
131	"	John Holmes,	British.
132	1827	John D. Anders,	American.
133	1835	Frederick L. Koelbing,	Continental.
134	"	John C. Bechler,	American.
135	1836	C. A. Pohlman,	British.
136	"	H. P. Halbeck,	South Africa.
137	"	Jacob Levin Reichel,	Continental.
138	"	Daniel F. Gambs,	"
139	"	William Henry Van Vleck,	American.
140	"	John King Martyn,	British.

No.	Year of Consecration.	Bishops.	Provinces.
141	1836	John Ellis,	West Indies.
142	1843	John M. Nitschman,	Continental.
143	"	C. C. Ultsch,	"
144	"	John Stengaerd,	"
145	1844	William Wisdom Essex,	British.
146	1845	Peter Wolle,	American.
147	1846	John G. Herman,	"
148	"	Benjamin Seifferth,	British.
149	1848	C. W. Matthiesen,	Continental.
150	1852	F. Joachim Nielsen,	" (Russia.)
151	"	John Rogers,	British.
152	1853	John C Breutel,	Continental.
153	"	Henry T. Dober,	"
154	"	George Wall Westerby,	West Indies.
155	1854	John Christian Jacobson,	American.
156	1857	Godfrey Andrew Cunow,	Continental.
157	"	William Edwards,	British.
158	"	Charles William Jahn,	Continental.
159	"	Henry Rudolph Wullschlaegel,	"
160	1858	Samuel Reinke,	American.

CHAPTER VI.

WORSHIP.

THE manner of worship, in all essential points, is uniform throughout the Provinces of the Unity and the Foreign Missions. It is based upon a Ritual, of which an abstract is given below, and which may be found at length in the first part of the "Liturgy and Hymns for the use of the Protestant Church of the United Brethren or Unitas Fratrum," and upon certain peculiar services of the church, to be described in this chapter.

DAYS AND SEASONS.

The Lord's Day is of divine appointment, and its solemn observance as a day of rest and worship, absolutely binding. It is particularly, but not exclusively, set apart for the ministrations of the Word and Sacraments.

Services in the Week.—Public services of various kinds are held on week-day evenings. In the Continental Province, and in some of the churches of the British, these services take place every evening in the week throughout the entire year.

Church Seasons.—The seasons and festivals of the

ecclesiastical year are observed, namely: Advent, Christmas, Epiphany, Lent, the Passion Week, Easter, Ascension-day, Whitsuntide, and Trinity Sunday.

Memorial Days.—Besides these seasons and festivals, the church has what are called "Memorial Days;" being the anniversaries of certain of the most important events in its early history. They are the following: January 19th, commencement of the mission among the heathen in Greenland, in the year 1733; March 1st, beginning of the Church of the Brethren, in the year 1457; May 12th, laying of the foundation-stone for the first church-edifice at Herrnhut, in the year 1724; and agreement to the first Statutes of the congregation there, in the year 1727; June 17th, beginning of the building of Herrnhut by the immigrants from Moravia, in the year 1722; July 6th, martyrdom of John Hus, in the year 1415; August 13th, the extraordinarily blessed celebration of the Holy Communion, in the parish church at Berthelsdorf, in the year 1727, whereby the new covenant of love and peace between the members of the congregation, entered into by the signing of the Statutes, on May 12th, was sealed, and a remarkable baptism of the Spirit granted; September 16th, the abolition of the office of Chief Elder in the church by the Synodical Conference assembled at London, in the year 1741, a memorial day particularly for the ministers and other servants of the Brethren's Unity; November 13th, powerful experience in the Brethren's

Unity, on the occasion of making known the abolition of this office, that *Jesus* only is the Chief Shepherd and Head of the Church.

These Memorial Days are generally noticed in the public services of the evening, or of the Lord's Day next following. In many churches, however, the 13th of August and the 13th of November, are celebrated as solemn festivals. As a general thing, each church also observes the Anniversary Day of its organization; and this celebration is denominated its "Congregation Festival."

THE RITUAL.

The Church Litany.

The public services of the Lord's day begin with the Litany, which is used, in several languages, in all the churches of the Unity, including those of the foreign mission field. In the Continental Province, a separate meeting is held at nine o'clock in the morning, when the prayers of the Litany are read; in the American Province, the Litany is generally prayed in connection with the morning preaching, as follows:

*LORD, have mercy upon us.
Christ, have mercy upon us.
Lord, have mercy upon us.
Christ, hear us.
Lord, Lord God, merciful and gracious, long-suffering

* In all the forms of Ritual given in this chapter, the lines in italics are responses on the part of the congregation.

and abundant in goodness and truth, keeping mercy for thousands, forgiving iniquity, and transgression, and sin, and that will by no means clear the guilty; (Exod. xxxiv 6, 7.)

Incline thine ear and hear: for we do not present our supplications before thee for our righteousnesses, but for thy great mercies. (Daniel ix. 18.)

Lord God, our FATHER which art in heaven,

Hallowed be thy name; thy kingdom come; thy will be done in earth, as it is in heaven; give us this day our daily bread; and forgive us our trespasses, as we forgive them that trespass against us; and lead us not into temptation, but deliver us from evil; for thine is the kingdom, and the power, and the glory, for ever and ever: Amen.

Lord God, SON, thou Saviour of the world.

Be gracious unto us.

Lord God, HOLY GHOST,

Abide with us forever.

Most holy blessed TRINITY.
We praise thee to eternity.

Thou LAMB once slain, our God and Lord,
To needy prayers thine ear afford,
And on us all have mercy.

From coldness to thy merits and death,
From error and misunderstanding,
From the loss of our glory in thee,
From the unhappy desire of becoming great,
From self-complacency,
From untimely projects,
From needless perplexity,
From the murdering spirit and devices of Satan,

From the influence of the spirit of this world,
From hypocrisy and fanaticism,
From the deceitfulness of sin,
From all sin,
Preserve us, gracious Lord and God.
By all the merits of thy life,
By thy human birth and circumcision,
By thy obedience, diligence, and faithfulness,
By thy humility, meekness, and patience,
By thy extreme poverty,
By thy holy baptism,
By thy watching, fasting, and temptations,
By thy griefs and sorrows,
By thy prayers and tears,
By thy having been despised and rejected,
Bless and comfort us, gracious Lord and God.
By thine agony and bloody sweat,
By thy bonds and scourgings,
By thy crown of thorns,
By thy cross and passion,
By thy sacred wounds and precious blood,
By thy dying words,
By thy atoning death,
By thy rest in the grave,
By thy glorious resurrection and ascension,
By thy sitting at the right hand of God,
By thy sending the Holy Ghost,
By thy prevailing intercession,
By the holy sacraments,
By thy divine presence, (Matt. xxviii. 20.)
By thy coming again to thy church on earth, or our being called home to thee,
Bless and comfort us, gracious Lord and God.

We humbly pray with one accord,
Remember us, most gracious Lord;
Think on thy sufferings, wounds, and cross,
And how by death thou savedst us;
For this is all our hope and plea,
In time and in eternity.

We poor sinners pray:
Hear us, gracious Lord and God.

Rule and lead the holy Christian church;

Increase the knowledge of the mystery of Christ, and diminish misapprehensions;

Make the word of the cross universal among those who are called by thy name;

Unite all the children of God in one spirit; (John xi. 52.)

Abide their only Shepherd, High-priest and Saviour;

Send faithful laborers into thy harvest; (Matt. ix. 38.)

Give spirit and power to preach thy word;

Preserve unto us the word of reconciliation till the end of days;

And through the Holy Ghost, daily glorify the merits of thy life, sufferings, and death:

Hear us, gracious Lord and God.

Prevent or destroy all designs and schemes of Satan, and defend us against his accusation; (Rev. xii. 10.)

For the sake of that peace which we have with thee, may we, as much as lieth in us, live peaceably with all men; (Rom. xii. 18.)

Grant us to bless them that curse us, and to do good to them that hate us; (Matt. v. 44.)

Have mercy upon our slanderers and persecutors, and lay not this sin to their charge; (Acts vii. 60.)

Hinder all schisms and offences;

Put far from thy people all deceivers and seducers;

Bring back those who have erred, or have been seduced;

Grant love and unity to all our congregations:

Hear us, gracious Lord and God.

Thou Light and Desire of all nations; (Matt. iv. 16; Hag. ii. 7.)

Watch over thy messengers both by land and sea;

Prosper the endeavors of all thy servants, to spread thy gospel among heathen nations;

Accompany the word of their testimony concerning thy atonement, with demonstration of the Spirit and of power; (1 Cor. ii. 4.)

Bless our and all other Christian congregations gathered from among the heathen;

Keep them as the apple of thine eye; (Deut. xxxii. 10.)

Have mercy on thy ancient covenant-people, the Jews; deliver them from their blindness; (Rom. xi. 25, 26.)

And bring all nations to the saving knowledge of thee:

Hear us, gracious Lord and God.

O praise the Lord, all ye heathen:
PRAISE HIM, ALL YE NATIONS.

Give to thy people open doors to preach the gospel, and set them to thy praise on earth; (Rev. iii. 8.)

Grant to all bishops and ministers of the church soundness of doctrine and holiness of life, and preserve them therein; (Tit. i. 7, ii. 1.)

Help all elders to rule well, especially those who labor in the word and doctrine; that they may feed thy church, which thou hast purchased with thine own blood: (1 Tim. v. 17; Acts xx. 28.)

Hear us, gracious Lord and God.

Watch graciously over all governments, and hear our intercessions for them; (1 Tim. ii. 1, 2.)

Grant and preserve unto them thoughts of peace and concord;

We beseech thee especially, to pour down thy blessings in a plentiful manner upon the President of the United States, and the Governors of the individual States of the Union; upon both Houses of Congress, and the respective State Legislatures, whenever assembled. Direct and prosper all their councils and undertakings to the promotion of thy glory, the propagation of the gospel, and the safety and welfare of this country.

Guide and protect the magistrates of the land wherein we dwell, and all that are put in authority; and grant us to lead under them a quiet and peaceable life, in all godliness and honesty: (1 Tim. ii. 2.)

Hear us, gracious Lord and God.

Teach us to submit ourselves to every ordinance of man for thy sake; and to seek the peace of the places where we dwell; (1 Pet. ii. 13; Jer. xxix. 7.)

Grant them blessing and prosperity;

Prevent war, and the effusion of human blood;

Preserve the land from distress by fire and water, hail and tempest, plague, pestilence, and famine;

Let the earth be like a field which the Lord blesseth;

Give peace and salvation, O God, to this land, and to all that dwell therein:

Hear us, gracious Lord and God.

TO BE PRAYED IN TIME OF WAR.

[Grant, O Lord, unto the President of the United States, in these times of danger, thy gracious counsel, that in all things he may approve himself the father of the people;

Be thou the gracious Protector of these States, and of our fellow-citizens in all parts of the world;

Turn the hearts of our enemies; defeat every evil design against us; and continue to show thy tender mercy unto these United States, as thou hast done in the days past;

Cause us to bow down before thee, to confess our sins, and to acknowledge with contrite hearts, that it is of thy mercies that we are not consumed; (Lam. iii. 22.)

Stop in thy tender mercy the effusion of human blood, and make discord and wars to cease;

To this end, put into the hearts of the rulers of the nations thoughts of peace, that we may see it soon established, to the glory of thy name:

Hear us, gracious Lord and God.]

Promote, we pray, thy servants' good,
Redeemed with thy most precious blood:
Among thy saints make us ascend
To glory that shall never end:
O Lord, have mercy on us all,
Have mercy on us when we call:
Lord, we have put our trust in thee,
Confounded let us never be; Amen.

Supply, O Lord, we pray thee, all the wants of thy Church:

Let all things be conducted among us in such a manner, that we provide things honest, not only in the sight of the Lord, but also in the sight of men; (2 Cor. viii. 21:)

Bless the sweat of the brow, and faithfulness in business:

Let none entangle himself with the affairs of this life; (2 Tim. ii. 4.)

But may all our labor of body and mind be hallowed unto thee:

Hear us, gracious Lord and God.

O thou Preserver of men, (Job vii. 20.)

Send help to all that are in distress or danger;

Strengthen and uphold those who suffer bonds and persecution for the sake of the gospel; (Heb. xiii. 3.)

Defend and provide for fatherless children and widows, and all who are desolate and oppressed; (Ps. lxviii. 5.)

Be the support of the aged; (Is. xlvi. 4.)

Make the bed of the sick, and, in the midst of suffering, let them feel that thou lovest them; (Ps. xli. 3.)

And when thou takest away men's breath, that they die, then remember, that thou hast died, not for our sins only, but also for the sins of the whole world; (1 John ii. 2; Rom. v. 18.)

Hear us, gracious Lord and God.

O Lord, thou who art over all, God blessed for ever, (Rom. ix. 5.)

Be the Saviour of all men; (1 Tim. iv. 10.)

Yea, have mercy on thy whole creation; (Rom. viii. 19, 22.)

For thou camest, by thyself to reconcile all things unto God, whether things in earth, or things in heaven; (Col. i. 20; Eph. ii. 16.)

Hear us, gracious Lord and God.

Thou, Saviour of thy body, the church, (Eph. v. 23.)

Bless, sanctify, and preserve every member, through the truth; (John xvii. 17.)

Grant that each, in every age and station, may enjoy the powerful and sanctifying merits of thy holy humanity; and make us chaste before thee in soul and body;

Let our children be brought up in thy nurture and admonition; (Eph. vi. 4.)

Pour out thy Holy Spirit on all thy servants and handmaids: (Acts ii. 18.)

Purify our souls in obeying the truth, through the Spirit unto unfeigned love of the brethren: (1 Pet. i. 22.)

Hear us, gracious Lord and God.

Keep us in everlasting fellowship with the church triumphant, and let us rest together in thy presence from our labors:

Hear us, gracious Lord and God.

O Christ, almighty God,

Have mercy upon us.

O thou Lamb of God, which takest away the sin of the world, (John i. 29.)

Own us to be thine.

O thou Lamb of God, which takest away the sin of the world,

Be joyful over us.

O thou Lamb of God which takest away the sin of the world,

Leave thy peace with us.

O Christ, hear us.

Lord, have mercy upon us.

Christ, have mercy upon us.

Lord, have mercy upon us.

DOXOLOGY—TO BE USED ON FESTAL OCCASIONS.

Unto the Lamb that was slain, (Rev. v. 12.)

And hath redeemed us out of all nations of the earth: (Rev. v. 9.)

Unto the Lord who purchased our souls for himself: (Acts xx. 28.)

Unto that Friend who loved us,—and washed us from our sins in his own blood: (Rev. i. 5.)

Who died for us once, (Rom. vi. 10, 11; 2 Cor. v. 15.)

That we might die unto sin; (1 Pet. ii. 24.)

Who rose for us,

That we also might rise; (1 Cor. xv.)

Who ascended for us into heaven,

To prepare a place for us; (John xiv. 2, 3.)

CHOIR. And to whom are subjected the angels, and powers, and dominions; (1 Pet. iii. 22.)

To him be glory at all times,

In the church that waiteth for him,—and in that which is around him,

CHOIR. From everlasting to everlasting: *Amen.*

MIN. Little children, abide in him; that when he shall appear, we may have confidence, and not be ashamed before him at his coming. (1 John ii. 28.)

> In none but him alone I trust for ever,
> In him, my Saviour.

The Lord bless thee, and keep thee;

The Lord make his face shine upon thee, and be gracious unto thee;

The Lord lift up his countenance upon thee, and give thee peace:

In the name of Jesus: Amen.

THE MINISTRATION OF BAPTISM TO INFANTS.

Baptism is to be administered with befitting solemnity, ordinarily in a public meeting of the congregation, which the children especially should attend. After the singing of a suitable hymn, and a short discourse, treating of the nature of baptism, and the obligations of parents presenting their children to be baptized, the congregation rises, and unites with the officiating minister in the following petitions:

CHRIST, thou Lamb of God, which takest away the sin of the world,

Leave thy peace with us: Amen.

By thy holy sacraments,

Bless us, gracious Lord and God.

Baptism is the answer of a good conscience towards God, who hath saved us by the washing of regeneration and renewing of the Holy Ghost, which is shed on us abundantly through Jesus Christ our Saviour.

Children, also, may be made partakers of this grace;

For Christ hath said, Suffer little children to come unto me, and forbid them not, for of such is the kingdom of heaven.

An infant we present to thee,
As thy redeemed property,
And thee most fervently entreat,
Thyself this child to consecrate
By baptism, and its soul to bless,
Out of the fulness of thy grace.

(The child having been brought in, the minister offers up a prayer.)

Ye who are baptized into Christ Jesus, how were ye baptized?

Into his death.

N. N., into the death of Jesus I baptize thee, in the name of the Father, and of the Son, and of the Holy Ghost.

(During the imposition of hands the minister continues:)

Now art thou buried with him by baptism into his death;

In the name of Jesus: Amen.

Now therefore live, yet not thou, but Christ live in thee; and the life which thou now livest in the flesh, live by the faith of the Son of God, who loved thee, and gave himself for thee.

This grant according to thy word,
Through Jesus Christ our only Lord,
O, Father, Son, and Spirit.

The Lord bless thee, and keep thee;

The Lord make his face shine upon thee, and be gracious unto thee;

The Lord lift up his countenance upon thee, and give thee peace;

In the name of Jesus: Amen.

A second Litany, to be used at the baptism of children, may be found in the first part of the Hymn Book, pages xviii. xix.

THE MINISTRATION OF BAPTISM TO ADULTS.

By the administration of Baptism, in the case of an adult, the person baptized is admitted to the communicant congregation. This sacrament, except illness prevents it, is always administered in a public meeting. The service begins with the following hymn:

Christ, the almighty Son of God,
Took on him human flesh and blood,
And willingly gave up his breath
To save us from eternal death.

Praise to the Father and the Son,
And Holy Spirit, Three in One,
That we're from condemnation free'd,
Since Christ our ransom fully paid.

[After a short discourse by the minister, follow these petitions :]

Lord God, our FATHER, which art in heaven,

Hallowed be thy name ; thy kingdom come ; thy will be done in earth as it is in heaven ; give us this day our daily bread ; and forgive us our trespasses, as we forgive them that trespass against us ; and lead us not into temptation, but deliver us from evil : for thine is the kingdom, and the power, and the glory, for ever and ever : Amen.

Lord God, SON, thou Saviour of the world,

Be gracious unto us.

Lord God, HOLY GHOST,

Abide with us forever.

Thou LAMB once slain, our God and Lord,
To needy prayers thine ear afford,
And on us all have mercy.

By thy divine presence,
By thy holy sacraments,
Bless us, gracious Lord and God.

[Then the minister puts the following questions to the candidate for baptism :]

Dost thou believe in God the Father, almighty Maker and Preserver of heaven and earth ?

ANSWER. *I do.*

Dost thou believe in Jesus Christ, the only begotten Son of God, our Lord, who loved us, and gave himself for us ?

ANSWER. *I do.*

Dost thou believe in the Holy Ghost, the holy Christian

church, the forgiveness of sins, the resurrection of the body, and the life everlasting?

ANSWER. *I do.*

Dost thou believe that thou art a sinful creature, deserving of wrath and eternal punishment?

ANSWER. *I verily believe it.*

Dost thou believe that Jesus Christ is thy Lord, who redeemed thee, a lost and undone human creature, from sin, from death, and from the power of the devil, with his innocent suffering and dying, and with his holy and precious blood?

ANSWER. *I verily believe it.*

Dost thou in this faith desire to be baptized into the death of Jesus, to be washed from thy sins, and to be embodied into the congregation of the faithful?

ANSWER. *This is my sincere desire.*

Dost thou in this faith renounce the service of sin and Satan, and determine to live under Christ in his kingdom, and serve him in holiness and righteousness all the days of thy life?

ANSWER. *I do most heartily, in the strength of Jesus Christ, my Lord, and of his Holy Spirit.*

Unto HIM, O Lamb of God,—Open thy salvation's treasure
In rich measure;—graciously HIS sins forgive,
HIM receive,—Grant HIM peace and consolation;
Join HIM to thy congregation,—As the purchase of thy death.

The water flowing from thy side,
Which by the spear was open'd wide,
Be now HIS bath; thy precious blood
Cleanse HIM, and bring HIM nigh to God.

[The candidate for baptism kneeling, the minister offers up a prayer.]

Ye who are baptized into Christ Jesus, how were ye baptized?

Into his death.

N. N., into the death of Jesus I baptize thee, in the name of the Father, and of the Son, and of the Holy Ghost.

[During the imposition of hands, the minister continues:]

Now art thou washed, justified and sanctified by the blood of Christ: therefore live, yet not thou, but Christ live in thee; and the life, which thou now livest in the flesh, live by the faith of the Son of God, who loved thee, and gave himself for thee.

Amen, Hallelujah, Hallelujah,
Amen, Hallelujah.

[Then, the congregation kneeling, the following verses may be sung:]

May Christ thee sanctify and bless,
His Spirit's seal on thee impress;
His body, torn with many a wound,
Preserve thy soul and body sound.

The Father, Son, and Holy Ghost,
Will thee protect, we humbly trust.

The Lord bless thee and keep thee;

The Lord make his face shine upon thee, and be gracious unto thee;

The Lord lift up his countenance upon thee, and give thee peace.

In the name of Jesus: Amen.

There is a particular service for the baptism of adults from the heathen. See first part of the Hymn Book, pages xxii.–xxiv.

THE ORDER FOR THE ADMINISTRATION OF THE LORD'S SUPPER.

[The service is opened by singing verses expressive of penitence and contrition of heart, after which a prayer for absolution is offered up. The congregation rising, a verse is sung, and the bread is consecrated by pronouncing the words of institution :]

"Our Lord Jesus Christ, the same night in which he was betrayed, took bread, and when he had given thanks, he brake it, and gave it to his disciples, and said : Take, eat: this is my body, which is given for you. This do in remembrance of me."

[The consecrated bread is then distributed by the minister and his assistants among the communicants, during the singing of hymns, treating principally of the sufferings and death of our Lord. After all the communicants have received the bread, the minister repeats the words :]

Our Lord Jesus Christ said, "Take, eat: this is my body, which is given for you."

[The congregation partake altogether, kneeling either in silent prayer, or while a verse is sung, expressive of the solemn act. The congregation rising, verses of thanksgiving are sung, after which the minister consecrates the wine by pronouncing the words :]

"After the same manner also our Lord Jesus Christ took the cup, when he had supped, gave thanks, and gave it to them saying: Drink ye all of it: this is my blood, the blood of the New Testament, which is shed for you and for many, for the remission of sins. This do ye, as oft as ye drink it, in remembrance of me."

[The minister then partaking of the consecrated cup, delivers it to his assistants, by whom it is administered to the congregation ;

during which time hymns are sung, treating of the remission of sins in the blood of Jesus, and of its healing and sanctifying power.

The service is continued with hymns, treating of brotherly love, communion with Christ, and thankfulness for his incarnation, passion, and death, and concluded with the blessing.]

THE RITE OF CONFIRMATION.

Persons baptized in their infancy, are solemnly confirmed in their baptismal covenant previous to reception into the communicant congregation. The order of services in administering the rite, is the following:

[After singing suitable hymns, the minister delivers a discourse to the congregation, and closes with an address to the candidates for confirmation. Then he proceeds to put to them the following questions:]

1. Do you believe in your heart, and confess with your mouth, the divine truths of the Holy Scriptures; will you abide by them, as the rule of your conduct in life, and the ground of your hope in death?

ANSWER. *Yes.*

2. Are you now prepared, as in the presence of God the omniscient, and of this congregation, solemnly to renew and confirm your baptismal covenant, and to seal it in the holy supper?

ANSWER. *I am.*

3. Do you believe in God the Father, Son and Holy Ghost, in whose name you have been baptized, and do you look for remission of your sins and acceptance with God, solely through his mercy, and the all-sufficient merits of our Lord Jesus Christ?

ANSWER. *Yes, by the grace of God.*

4. Do you solemnly promise, anew, with a true heart and full purpose of soul, to renounce the world and sin, and to cleave with all your mind and strength to Christ your Saviour; by keeping his commandments, to fulfil your duties towards God and your neighbor, and thus in word and deed to honor and glorify your blessed Redeemer?

ANSWER. *Yes, God helping me.*

[The candidates having answered these questions, kneel down, and the minister imparts to each the blessing of confirmation, with imposition of hands, pronouncing at the same time a text of Scripture, such as :]

"The very God of peace sanctify you wholly; and I pray God your whole spirit, and soul, and body, be preserved blameless unto the coming of our Lord Jesus Christ." (1 Thess. v. 23.)

Or, "Now the God of peace, that brought again from the dead our Lord Jesus, that great Shepherd of the sheep, through the blood of the everlasting covenant, make you perfect in every good work to do his will, working in you that which is well-pleasing in his sight, through Jesus Christ." (Heb. xiii. 20, 21.)

[After this the minister adds :]

The Lord bless thee, and keep thee;

The Lord make his face shine upon thee, and be gracious unto thee;

The Lord lift up his countenance upon thee, and give thee peace;

In the name of Jesus : Amen.

[All then kneel down, and the persons confirmed are commended in prayer to the Lord. The service is concluded with a hymn.

All candidates for confirmation are, previous to it, carefully instructed by the minister in the doctrines of Christianity, with a particular reference to the Lord's Supper, of which they are invited to partake at the next celebration of this holy ordinance, subsequent to their confirmation.]

THE RITE OF ORDINATION.

[The service being opened by the singing of the hymn: Come, Holy Ghost, come Lord our God, &c., or some other suitable verses, the Bishop addresses the congregation in an appropriate discourse, ending with a charge to the candidate (or candidates) for ordination, after which he offers up a prayer, imploring the blessing of God upon the solemn transaction, and commending the candidate (or candidates) to his grace, that he may be endowed with power, and unction, and the influences of the Holy Ghost, for preaching the word of God, administering the holy sacraments, and for doing all those things which shall be committed unto him for the promotion of the spiritual edification of the church. The Bishop then proceeds to ordain the candidate (or candidates) with imposition of hands, pronouncing the following or similar words :]

I ordain (*consecrate*) thee, N. N., to be a Deacon (Presbyter) (Bishop) of the church of the United Brethren in the name of the Father, and of the Son, and of the Holy Ghost: *The Lord bless thee, and keep thee; The Lord make his face shine upon thee, and be gracious unto thee; The Lord lift up his countenance upon thee, and give thee peace: In the name of Jesus: Amen.*

[The Bishop having returned to his place, kneels down with the whole congregation, all worshipping in silent devotion; and after a suitable pause, one of the following DOXOLOGIES is sung by the choir, the congregation joining in the AMEN, HALLELUJAH.

The service is concluded with a short hymn, and the Bishop pronouncing the New Testament blessing.

N. B. At the consecration of Bishops, two, or three Bishops generally assist.

DOXOLOGIES.

(a) *To be used at the ordination of Deacons.*

Glory be to thy most meritorious MINISTRY,
O thou SERVANT of the true tabernacle,
Who did not come to be ministered unto,
But to minister.
Amen, Hallelujah, Hallelujah,
Amen, Hallelujah.

(b) *To be used at the Ordination of Presbyters.*

Glory be to thy most holy PRIESTHOOD,
CHRIST, thou LAMB OF GOD;
Thou who wast slain for us;
Who by one offering hast perfected for ever them that are sanctified.
Amen, Hallelujah, Hallelujah,
Amen, Hallelujah.

(c) *To be used at the Consecration of Bishops.*

Glory be to the SHEPHERD and BISHOP of our souls.
The great SHEPHERD of the sheep, through the blood of the everlasting covenant;
Glory and obedience be unto GOD the HOLY GHOST, our Guide and Comforter;
Glory and adoration be to the FATHER of our LORD JESUS CHRIST,
Who is the FATHER of all who are called children on earth and in heaven.

O might each pulse thansgiving beat,
And every breath His praise repeat.

Amen, Hallelujah, Hallelujah,
Amen, Hallelujah.

THE FORM OF SOLEMNIZATION OF MATRIMONY.

[The Minister says:]

Dearly Beloved: We are here assembled in the presence of God and this congregation, (company,) to join together this man, N. N., and this woman, N. N., in holy matrimony, which is declared by the Apostle to be honorable among all men; and, therefore, is not by any to be entered into unadvisedly or lightly, but reverently, discreetly, and in the fear of God. In this holy estate, these two persons are now to be united.

In holy writ we are taught:

That matrimony was instituted by God himself, and is, therefore, an holy estate;

That, according to the ordinance of God, a man and his wife shall be one flesh;

That what God hath joined together, man may not put asunder;

That, under the New Covenant, the married state hath been sanctified, to be an emblem of Christ and his church;

That the husband, as the head of the wife, should love her, even as Christ also loved the church; and that the wife be subject to her own husband in the Lord, as the church is subject unto Christ;

That, in consequence, Christians thus united together, should love one another, as one in the Lord, be faithful one to the other, assist each other mutually, and never forsake one another. Loving God, our Saviour, above all things, whatsoever they do, in word or deed, they should do all to the glory of God, and in the name of Jesus Christ.

Premising that there is no impediment to prevent your being lawfully joined together in wedlock, according to the word of God, and the laws of this country, I now ask thee, N. N.,

Wilt thou have this woman, N. N., here present, to thy wedded wife, to live together after God's ordinance, in the holy estate of matrimony? Wilt thou love her, honor her, and care for her; and, through the grace of God, approve thyself unto her, in every respect, as a faithful Christian husband, so long as ye both shall live?

ANSWER. *Yes.*

In like manner, I now ask thee, N. N.,

Wilt thou have this man, N. N., here present, to thy wedded husband, to live together, after God's ordinance, in the holy estate of matrimony? Wilt thou love him, honor him, and be subject unto him in the Lord; and through the grace of God, approve thyself unto him, in every respect, as a faithful Christian wife, so long as ye both shall live?

ANSWER. *Yes.*

For as much, then, as ye have thus consented to live together in holy wedlock, and have witnessed the same before God and this congregation (company,) we exhort you, that ye enter upon the estate of matrimony in the name of the Lord, and that ye live therein according to the precepts of his holy word.

To this end, we now unite with you, in imploring his divine aid and blessing, and the guidance and sanctification of his good Spirit.

Let us pray:

O Lord, our God! who thyself has instituted and blessed the estate of matrimony, sanctifying the same, under the new Covenant, to be an emblem of Christ and his church, we beseech thee, graciously to look upon these two persons, who are about to be united in holy wedlock. Grant, that they may enter upon, and continue in this estate, in thy name. Replenish their hearts with thy love, and enable them to be faithful one to the other, and thus to live together in perfect love and peace. Sanctify and bless their union; vouchsafe unto them the guidance of thy holy Spirit, and teach them to do that, which is well pleasing in thy sight, through Jesus Christ, our Lord. *Amen.*

[Here the minister joins their right hands.]

In the name of God, the Father, the Son, and the Holy Ghost, ye are now joined together, to live in holy wedlock, as husband and wife. Receive ye the blessing of the Lord:

The Lord bless you, and keep you;

The Lord make his face shine upon you, and be gracious unto you;

The Lord lift up his countenance upon you, and give you peace: *Amen.*

THE ORDER OF THE BURIAL OF THE DEAD.

When the funeral procession has reached the grave, the corpse is placed aside of it, and the minister says:

LORD, have mercy upon us.

Christ, have mercy upon us.

Lord, have mercy upon us.

Christ, hear us.

Lord God our FATHER which art in heaven,

Hallowed be thy name; thy kingdom come; thy will be done in earth, as it is in heaven: give us this day our daily bread; and forgive us our trespasses, as we forgive them that trespass against us; and lead us not into temptation;

but deliver us from evil: for thine is the kingdom, and the power, and the glory, for ever and ever: Amen.

Lord God, SON, thou Saviour of the world,

Be gracious unto us.

By thy human birth,
By thy prayers and tears,
By all the troubles of thy life,
By the grief and anguish of thy soul,
By thine agony and bloody sweat,
By thy bonds and scourgings,
By thy crown of thorns,
By thine ignominious crucifixion,
By thy sacred wounds and precious blood,
By thy atoning death,
By thy rest in the grave,
By thy glorious resurrection and ascension,
By thy sitting at the right hand of God,
By thy divine presence,
By thy coming again to thy church on earth, or our being called home to thee,

Bless and comfort us, gracious Lord and God.

Lord God, HOLY GHOST,

Abide with us for ever.

I am the Resurrection and the Life, saith the Lord; he that believeth in me, though he were dead, yet shall he live. And whosoever liveth and believeth in me shall never die.

Therefore, blessed are the dead which die in the Lord from henceforth; yea, saith the Spirit, that they may rest from their labors.

O death, where is thy sting? O grave, where is thy victory? The sting of death is sin, and the strength of sin is the law: but thanks be to God, which giveth us the victory through our Lord Jesus Christ. *Amen.*

Now to the earth let these remains,
In hope committed be;
Until the body chang'd attains
To immortality.

[During the singing of this verse, the corpse is committed to the grave.]

We poor sinners pray,

Hear us, gracious Lord and God;

And keep us in everlasting fellowship with the church triumphant, and let us rest together in thy presence from our labors. *Amen.*

None of us liveth to himself, and no man dieth to himself; for whether we live, we live unto the Lord, and whether we die, we die unto the Lord; whether we live therefore or die, we are the Lord's: for to this end Christ both died, and rose, and revived, that he might be Lord both of the dead and living.

Blessed and holy is he that hath part in the first resurrection: on such the second death hath no power, but they shall be priests of God and of Christ.

Glory be to Him who is the Resurrection and the Life, who quickeneth us, while in this dying state, and after we have obtained the true life, doth not suffer us to die any more.

Glory be to Him in the church which waiteth for Him, and in that which is around Him, for ever and ever. *Amen.*

The Saviour's blood and righteousness,
My beauty is, my glorious dress;
Thus well array'd I need not fear,
When in his presence I appear.

The grace of our Lord Jesus Christ, the Love of God, and the Communion of the Holy Ghost, be with us all. *Amen.*

A second Burial-Litany may be found in the first part of the Hymn Book, pages xxxi. and xxxii.

Prayer Meetings.—The Monthly Concert for Prayer, on the first Monday of the month, is held in all the Provinces, on which occasion, in fellowship with many other children of God, the work of the Lord in heathen lands is particularly made the subject of supplications. Besides this stated service, other prayer meetings are frequently held, and conducted in various ways in the different Provinces and churches.

PECULIAR SERVICES.

Love-Feasts.—Love-Feasts, which are derived from the Agapæ of the apostolical church, are celebrated on various occasions, generally in connection with a solemn festival, or preparatory to the Holy Communion. The service consists in singing hymns and anthems, alternately, by the choir and congregation. Printed odes are often used, prepared expressly for the occasion. In the course of the service a simple meal of biscuit and coffee or tea, is served, of which the congregation partake together. In some churches the Love-Feast concludes with an address by the minister.

Liturgical Services.—These are either so called

"Liturgies," or "Singing-Meetings." On occasion of the former, a printed collection of hymns and anthems of praise is used, which are sung or chanted, alternately, by the minister, choir and congregation. The latter are conducted as follows: the minister selects a number of verses from different hymns, in such a manner that the whole series sets forth a connected view of some devotional subject; so that the congregation, while singing, may feel as deep an interest in it, and contemplate it as directly as though listening to a discourse. They are thus "speaking to themselves in psalms, and hymns, and spiritual songs, singing and making melody in their hearts to the Lord." (Ephes. v. 18, 19.) These Liturgical Services, which are very edifying, are confined, in the American Province, almost exclusively to German churches.

Services on Christmas Eve and New Year's Eve.—On Christmas Eve a solemn service is held, commemorating the birth of Christ. The narrative of the event is read from the gospels; hymns and anthems are sung by the choir and congregation; an address is delivered; and prayers are offered up. On New Year's Eve there are generally two services. The first, in some congregations, is a Love-Feast; in others it is devoted to the reading of the Pastor's Annual Report. The second service begins half an hour before midnight. On this occasion the minister delivers a suitable discourse, and continues speaking until precisely at twelve o'clock, the organ, accompanied by a corps of trombonists, peals forth in its loudest notes, announcing the New Year; the congregation rising at the same time, and singing the following hymn of thanksgiving:—

Now let us praise the Lord
  With body, soul, and spirit;
Who doth such wondrous things,
  Beyond our sense and merit;
Who from our mother's womb,
  And earliest infancy,
Hath done great things for us;
  Praise him eternally.

O, gracious God, bestow
  On us, while here remaining,
An ever cheerful mind;
  Thy peace be ever reigning.
Preserve us in true faith,
  And Christian holiness;
That when we go from hence,
  We may behold thy face.

Immediately afterward the congregation kneels in prayer, and the minister invokes the blessing of the Lord, for the new year, upon the authorities, ministers and congregations of the Moravian Church, the foreign missions, and all its other enterprises, the government of the country, the Church of Christ generally, in all its parts, and the whole world. Thereupon the Scripture texts, appointed in the Text Book of the church for the first day of the new year, are read, and the service is concluded with a hymn and the benediction.

Services of the Passion Week and Easter Festival.— The Passion Week, beginning with the Saturday before Palm Sunday, and extending to the following Saturday, is observed in a peculiarly solemn manner. In the evening of the first Saturday, a series of services commence, which are continued throughout the week, and have for their object the commemoration of the events in the history of the last days of the Son of Man, from the time when Jesus was anointed "for his burial," by Mary, at Bethany, to the day on which his body was laid in the tomb. In order to this commemoration, the history is read from a harmony of the four Gospels, published by the Church. At appropriate passages the reading is varied by hymns relating to what has been read, or by chants and anthems of the choir; at other passages prayer is offered up. On Palm Sunday the rite of Confirmation is administered, and on Maundy Thursday evening the Holy Communion celebrated. Good Friday is distinguished by several services, conducted in the manner stated above; and on the afternoon of the Saturday before Easter, a Love-Feast is celebrated. At sunrise on Easter Sunday, the resurrection of the Lord from the grave is commemorated by a solemn worship, on which occasion the Easter Morning Litany (see chapter on Doctrine) is used. This service, wherever it is practicable, takes place on the church burying-ground, to which the congregation moves in procession, preceded by a corps of trombonists and singers.

The manner of observing the Passion Week is the same in all the Provinces and mission fields of the Unity.

CHAPTER VII.

DISCIPLINE.

The Brethren of the Renewed Church, in accordance with the example of the apostolical churches, and of the Ancient Unitas Fratrum, established a Church Discipline at an early day of their history. This Discipline they considered of very great importance. When the Saxon government sent commissioners to Herrnhut, in order to examine the doctrines and constitution of the congregation there, the Brethren declared their readiness to forsake all they had, and go into other lands, if the free exercise of their Discipline were not conceded. Since that time the Discipline has continued unchanged in its fundamental principles. These are committed to the safe keeping of the General Synod, whose duty it is, through its Executive Board, to care for their observance in all parts of the Unity. At the same time, however, each Province, and each church in the same, as well as the Foreign Mission Provinces, all have respectively a Discipline of their own, based upon these fundamental principles.

In this chapter the principles are given, as set forth in the "Synodal Results;" and then the more particular rules for the American Province.

NATURE AND PURPOSE OF CHURCH DISCIPLINE.

By the term Church Discipline, taken in its widest sense, the church understands a training of its members for their calling of grace. To effect this, one of the most important means is a faithful care of souls, on the part of pastors; whose duty it is to visit the members of their congregations, encourage friendly intercourse with themselves, and minister to the spiritual necessities of every soul. In a more limited sense of the word, Church Discipline denótes the various degrees of brotherly correction which are employed, when affectionate admonitions prove fruitless; according to the directions given in Matt. xviii. 15, 17; 1 Cor. v. 11, 13; 1 Tim. vi. 3, 5; 2 John verse 10.

The purpose of Church Discipline is a two-fold one. By it, in the first place, the Christian character of an entire congregation is to be strictly maintained; and, in the second place, individual members are to be guarded from giving offence and falling into sin; to be kept in the way of righteous, sober and holy living; and to be restored in the spirit of meekness, when any have departed from this way.

EXERCISE OF CHURCH DISCIPLINE.

1. In its widest signification, Church Discipline is exercised by means of the public proclamation of the Divine Word; as well as by the mutual fraternal

admonitions and warnings of the members of a congregation. Brotherly love precedes all discipline and constitutes its very source. The first object of this love must be the spiritual welfare of the members of a congregation. "If a man be overtaken in a fault, restore such an one in the spirit of meekness." (Gal. vi. 1.) Words spoken in kindness, even though they convey a reproof, may find, by the grace of God, access to the heart;—then "thou hast gained thy brother." When transgressions occur, in a congregation, of such a nature that they ought to be reported to the Pastor, or his advisory Board or Committee, it becomes the duty of every member, who is acquainted with the circumstances, to render a timely exercise of discipline possible, by a candid and truthful communication. At the same time, every thing like tale-bearing or calumny, which are ranked in Scripture with heinous sins, is to be carefully guarded against. In order to prove the truth of a charge, and especially when the individual accused denies it, the name of the informant must be given, and an opportunity afforded for both parties to meet in the presence of the Pastor. With such cases, the exercise of Church Discipline in the restricted sense begins.

2. There are three degrees of Church Discipline understood in this sense.

The first consists in reproof administered by the Pastor to those who have erred, in accordance with the duty which his office imposes upon him before the

Lord. At such times he must admonish and rebuke with earnestness and fidelity, with humility and true affection.

In the event of graver transgressions, especially when they have become open and manifest, the second degree of Church Discipline must be put in force. It consists in summoning the delinquent before the Board of Elders or the Standing Committee of a congregation, (see below,) in accordance with the injunction of the Lord: "If thy brother will not hear thee, then take with thee one or two more, that in the presence of two or three witnesses, every word may be established." (Mat xviii. 16.) After having examined the delinquent, this Board, in connection with the Pastor, is to decide whether he shall be suspended from the Lord's Supper, or not. Such suspension may be resorted to in particular cases, instead of excommunication, even where open offence has been given by sinful practices; but only if unfeigned repentance is manifested, and a real change of heart may be hoped for.

The third and last degree of Church Discipline is excommunication. This is to be resorted to in case no change takes place after milder measures have been used, but the erring member continues in his evil ways, obstinately resisting the rules of the church, and proving a stumbling block to others; and in the case of such as fall into gross sins, whereby the name of Christ is evil spoken of, according to the rule of the apostle: "put away from among you that wicked person." (Cor. v. 13.) In exercising this and the second degree of discipline, compassionate love must prevail, but not personal considerations or a false tenderness. It becomes the solemn duty of the Board of Elders to proceed in every case with the utmost conscientiousness, impartially weighing all circumstances, and earnestly praying for the guidance of the Holy Spirit. Cases of excommunication are to be announced to the communicant congregation, at a suitable meeting.

RE-ADMISSION.

It is the province of the Board of Elders, in connection with the Pastor, to determine the time for the re-admission of such as have been suspended from the Lord's Supper, or excluded from the church; and they must act in this matter with the greatest circumspection. The state of heart of the candidate for re-admission, and not external considerations of any kind, must guide them in their decision. Cases of re-admission to the church are also to be announced to the communicant congregation.

RULES FOR INDIVIDUAL CHURCHES.

The several churches, as was stated before, have particular rules for their own government, based upon the principles of Discipline which are common to the whole Unity. These rules must contain nothing which is contrary to the decrees of the General Synod or of the Provincial Synod, under which a church stands.

For the American Province the following regulations have been established by its Synods :

I. *The Necessity of Rules.*

1. Every individual church is bound to profess adherence to a written or printed code of regulations, embodying its own particular constitution and discipline, and commonly denominated "A Brotherly Agreement."

2. This code must be in accordance with the principles of the constitution and general discipline, laid down by the General Synod, and the Provincial Synod, and contain nothing contrary to the enactments of either.

3. Every church is at liberty, either to prepare a draft of such a code, to be laid before the Provincial Elders' Conference, for its sanction, modification or rejection ; or to request the Provincial Elders' Conference to furnish a draft. In the latter case, the church may propose amendments, reject the whole, and substitute a new draft ; always, however, subject to the revision and approval of the Provincial Elders' Conference. If necessary, a delegation may be sent to confer with this Conference on the subject. As soon as the Provincial Elders' Conference has expressed its sanction, in writing, the rules may be adopted by the church.

II. *Officers administering the Rules.*

1. Every church elects a Committee, called either the "Board of Elders," or the "Standing Committee," whose duty it is to aid the Pastor in the government of that church.

2. To this body, in some churches, the financial affairs are also entrusted; in others, these are managed by a second and distinct Board, called the "Board of Trustees."

3. The position which the Pastor holds in the "Board of Elders," or the "Standing Committee," is determined by each particular church, and depends, in the case of those churches which are incorporated, on the provisions of their charters.

4. In spiritual matters, however, and those relating to public worship, the "Board of Elders," or the "Standing Committee," can, in no case, act independently of the Pastor.

5. It is the duty of this Board, in conjunction with the Pastor, to see that the rules which govern the Brethren's Unity generally, and those which refer to the Province, as well as the particular rules of the church over which the Board is placed, are faithfully observed.

III. *Relation of the Officers of a Church to the Provincial Elders' Conference.*

1. The Pastor of a church, the Chairman of the "Board of Elders," or the "Standing Committee,"

(in those cases where this office is distinct from the Pastor's,) and every member of the same, are subject to the Provincial Elders' Conference, and bound to respect and obey its constitutional enactments.

2. The Provincial Elders' Conference only appoints Pastors to churches. The Board of a church may propose a Pastor, with the full understanding, however, that the Provincial Elders' Conference is not bound to respect such propositions any further than it may deem proper.

3. The Board of a church may decline to receive a Pastor appointed by the Provincial Elders' Conference; but cannot prevent the removal of a stationed Pastor, if the Provincial Elders' Conference gives him another appointment.

4. In case a Pastor has lost the confidence of his church, the Board of the same is authorized to report the fact to the Provincial Elders' Conference, which body, after a thorough investigation, is to act in the matter according to its conscientious convictions.

5. Complaints against a Pastor, or any other ministerial servant of the church, must be lodged with the Provincial Elders' Conference, which body is bound to inform him of the name of his accuser, if he desires to know it.

6. The Boards of the respective churches, as well as their members generally, have petitionary powers with respect to the Provincial Elders' Conference; but all petitions directed to this Conference must be couched in respectful terms, and evidence a brotherly disposition.

IV. *General Meetings of a Church.*

1. On business of importance, or general interest, a meeting of the church is called. Such a meeting is usually denominated a "Church Council."

2. The organization of this Council depends on the rules and regulations of the church which holds it.

3. In all matters relating to an individual church, said church determines—and if it is incorporated, according to its charter—who shall be voting members of the Council, and the manner of voting.

4. In the election of delegates to the Provincial Synod, however, and all other matters affecting the entire Province, the manner of voting, and the qualifications for voting, are regulated by the enactments of the Provincial Synod, and the Council is bound to obey these. The enactments in the case of the election of delegates, are set forth by the Provincial Elders' Conference in their circular, issued previous to each election.

CORRECTION.

On page 51, an incorrect statement occurs, in the second sentence of Section I. That sentence should read: "To the latter belong the Moravian churches in North Carolina, and one in Virginia; to the former, all the rest in the United States." And on page 54, "Mount Bethel, organized in 1851," should appear as located in Virginia, and not in North Carolina. On page 71, in the list of the churches of the British Province, *Greengates*, a congregation affiliated to Baildon, has been omitted.

STATISTICAL APPENDIX.

The statistics here presented are altogether summary, and intended to give merely a general view of the numerical condition of the church. Detailed statistics, which change very much every year, belong to the periodical publications of the church, and not to a Manual like this. The statistics of the Foreign Mission work are given somewhat more fully than the rest, because this enterprise is one of particular interest, and frequent inquiries are made respecting it. In compiling these statistics, the reports for the year 1858 were used. The writer is not certain whether he has given the correct number of communicants in the Continental Province; the statistics which were sent him from Germany did not distinguish between communicants and the whole number of souls. Hence he substracted the whole number of children, and one half the number of those designated as youths and maidens, from the whole number of souls, and gave the remainder as the number of communicants in that Province; inasmuch as all persons are there confirmed when they reach the age of fifteen or sixteen years.

I. THE HOME CHURCH.

	Communicants.	Whole No. including children.
American Province, Northern District, 4,285* Southern District, 1,015	5,300	8,275
Continental Province.........	4,677	6,174
British Province...............	2,980	5,184
Total..........................	12,947	19,633

* Including the communicants of the Home Mission Churches.

II. THE CONTINENTAL DIASPORA.*

	No. of cities, towns and villages visited.	Members of Societies.	Members of the Diaspora.
A.			
Germany..	1,965	1,494	11,153
Switzerland and France.	217	604	1,724
Denmark, Norway and Sweden	366	342	2,200
Total	2,548	2,440	15,077
B. Russian Empire.	Number of Parishes.	Number of Chapels.	Members of the Diaspora.
Livonia	35	109	19,721
Esthonia	26	126	42,364
St. Petersburg		1	200
Poland			2,000
Total	61	266	64,285
Total number of members of the Diaspora on the Continent			79,362

* The statistics of the Diaspora are incomplete, especially so far as the number of members of the Societies is concerned. In the report sent us from Germany, the number of these members in the Russian Empire, was not given. It must amount to many thousands. For explanations of this table, the reader is referred to pages 66 and 67.

III. THE FOREIGN MISSION FIELD.

Provinces.	Regular Stations.	No. of Missionaries.	Races and Tribes.	Communicants.	Baptized Adults.	Baptized Children.	Total Church fellowship	Candidates for Baptism, New People, and Excluded.	Total of Converts under Religious Instruction.
Greenland,	4	25	Esquimaux,	803	296	604	1,703	232	1,935
Labrador,	4	29	Esquimaux,	372	282	403	1,057	147	1,204
Canada and U.States,	5	9	Indians,	149	143	108	400	39	439
Mosquito Coast,	3	7	Indians and Negroes,	24	5	106	135	84	219
Danish West Indies,	8	28	Negroes,	3,297	508	3,024	6,829	2,913	9,742
Jamaica,	13	32	Negroes,	4,073	871	4,639	10,033	2,214	12,247
Antigua,	7	23	Negroes,	3,797	789	2,681	7,267	782	8,049
St. Kitts,	4	10	Negroes,	1,233	415	1,335	2,983	620	3,603
Barbadoes,	4	11	Negroes,	950	281	1,252	2,483	388	2,871
Tobago,	2	6	Negroes,	752	211	639	1,602	159	1,761
South America,	10	60	Negroes,	2,767	6,387	4,033	13,187	11,736	24,923
South Africa,	8	60	Hottentots, Kaffres, Fingoos, Tambookies,	1,976	1,285	2,642	5,903	1,417	7,545
Thibet,	1	3	Thibetans,	–	–	–	–	–	New enterprise commenced in 1856.
Australia,	1	2	Papuans,	–	–	–	–	–	New enterprise commenced in 1858.
Total,	74	305		20,193	11,473	21,916	53,582	20,731	74,538

IV. COMPARATIVE STATISTICS OF THE FOREIGN MISSION FIELD IN 1831 AND 1858.*

	1831.	1858.	Increase.
Stations	42	74	32
Missionaries	208	305	97
Communicants	15,800	20,193	4,393
Converts	43,600	74,538	30,938

V. CHURCH BOARDING SCHOOLS.

	Number of Schools.	Annual average of Scholars.	Teachers.
American Province	4	615	92
Continental Province	25	1,041	205
British Province	15	375	60
	44	2,031	357

* The increase in the last two years was 4 stations, 5 missionaries, 610 communicants, 866 baptized adults, 671 baptized children, 2,147 in church fellowship, and 3,191 converts under regular religious instruction.

www.ingramcontent.com/pod-product-compliance
Lightning Source LLC
LaVergne TN
LVHW011229110826
845150LV00006B/1582

9781425515164